WOW Woman Of Worth

**Women's Wellness:
Aging at Any Age with Moxie!**

Christine Awram

Published by Inspire Higher Consulting Inc. March 2020
ISBN: 9781777109004

Editor: Danielle Anderson
Typeset: Greg Salisbury
Book Cover Design: Judith Mazari

This book is dedicated to Kristal Barrett-Stuart, one of the most tenacious warriors of wellness that I'm privileged to know. Challenged by ongoing complications of Lyme disease, she continues to seek solutions while embracing everything she is grateful for. Even in the midst of significant suffering, she expresses heartfelt love and appreciation everywhere she goes. Kristal embodies every beautiful quality of a Woman Of Worth.

I have never met anyone with such a deeply rooted core of grace as you, dear Kristal, and I dedicate this book to you with prayers for your complete return to health. I love you my friend.

Christine Awram, Founder
Woman Of Worth WOW Worldwide

The WOW Credo

I am a Woman Of Worth
My worthiness is inherent and infinite –
    it is my natural state
My value is a reflection of who I AM –
    and I am magnificent
Who I am always makes a difference –
    because I MATTER
I am successful –
    coming from my true power which lies within
I am empowered –
    making choices from the clarity of my heart, mind and
    spirit
I am an empowered leader –
    impacting others from quiet acts of kindness to
    leading a nation
I am abundant –
    manifesting success from my core values
I cherish my relationships –
    they are part of what makes me strong
I am a Human BEing –
    as my BEing is of far more significance than my
    DOing
I play, laugh, and bring beauty and light into the world –
    I am RADIANT
At times I despair and I weep –
    when I feel the pain of a world that has momentarily
    gone mad
Yet even when I tremble through a dark night of the soul,
    I renew my faith and my courage in a single heartbeat
    because my spirit is indomitable
I feel, and I care, and I am passionately alive –
    with a heart as open as the universe

I AM A WOMAN OF WORTH, AND I AM GLORIOUS

"A Taste of WOW" – Your FREE Book is Waiting

This eBook includes five chapters: one from each book in the original WOW Series, to give you a taste of the powerful and heartfelt writing of our authors. Topics include Moms in Business, Empowered Entrepreneurs, The Power of Collaboration, Life & Leadership with Soul, and Mental Health Matters.

Get your free copy of
"A Taste of WOW" here:

www.awomanofworth.com/books

Acknowledgements

This entire book could be filled with the names of all the people I want to thank, for the many ways you've all helped inspire this book to become a reality. Heartfelt gratitude to the tremendous community I call my WOW Tribe. You rock.

To the fabulous females who are this book's contributing authors, you have staggered me with your willingness to show up 100%. Each and every one of you share my burning desire to make our world a more joyful and empowered place, and you've been the most courageous and extraordinary women to collaborate with. It has been an honour.

To my publisher Julie Salisbury, for taking my hand every step of the way while sharing your brilliance and making this adventure fun. You shine a very bright light my friend.

To our brilliant editor Danielle Anderson and meticulous typesetter Greg Salisbury, you pull all the pieces together to make our books shine even brighter. And to our graphic designer Judith Mazari, your covers add impact.

To my family and closest friends, you are the inner circle of my Tribe. I have no words to express how grateful I am for your love, and that you always have my back.

And especially to David Samuelson, my beloved Manly Man. You always believe in me, and see the best in me. I couldn't have done this without your love, faith and support. You are my heart.

Contents

Introduction: Christine Awram...XI

Living My Bold, Audacious Life: Lorna Ketler 1

Cross That Finish Line and Liberate Your Inner Champion: Gail Thevarge.. 13

Claiming My Truths – Moxie, Mayhem, and Magic: Ange Frymire 25

Turning My Curse Into My Blessing: Jennifer Desloges 39

Finding the Humour in Aging: Terry Jackson 53

My Screaming Hormones: Helen Horwat... 67

Live Young as Old as Possible: Marlies White... 81

Disconnected Motherhood CAN Be Reversed: Michelle Berezan 95

The Best is Yet to Come: Kristy Henkes-Joe.. 109

Just Say Yes!: Amy Hadikin... 123

Pause. Breathe. Shift.: Tammy Scarlett 135

Change – It's What We Do: Jocelyn Johnston... 149

A Recipe for Vibrant Beauty: DeeAnn Lensen 163

Your Health is In Your Hands … and Your Hips!: Janice Benna 177

Finding a Way Forward: Ali Perry-Davies 189

Introduction

by Christine Awram, Founder
Woman Of Worth WOW Worldwide

"Courage is looking fear right in the eye and saying, 'Get the hell out of my way, I've got things to do.'"
Author Unknown

Introduction

By Christine Awram, Founder
Woman Of Worth WOW Worldwide

*"Life should not be a journey to the grave with the intention
of arriving safely in a pretty and well-preserved body, but
rather to skid in broadside in a cloud of smoke, thoroughly
used up, totally worn out, and loudly proclaiming
"Wow! What a ride!"*
Hunter S. Thompson

"Will you marry me?"

I was in Las Vegas on the High Roller, the largest
observation wheel in the world, when I was blindsided by
these words. From a distance the High Roller looks like a giant
ferris wheel, but each "seat" is actually an enclosed capsule with
tall windows that can fit up to fifty people inside. There were

about a dozen of us rising high in the sky together, and as we reached the pinnacle of five-hundred feet, with the fairyland of a city that never sleeps laid out below, my beloved Manly Man dropped to one knee and whipped out a box from Tiffany's. A band of diamonds was twinkling at me, along with his beautiful blue eyes, and my mind went absolutely blank.

I didn't see this coming and was quite frankly gobsmacked. I'd be turning sixty in just a few weeks and had never been married. David (also known as Manly Man) and I had been together for thirteen years, we'd lived together as common-law partners for five, and he was my heart. But who gets married for the first time at sixty?

Moxie [def]:
"Vigor, nerve, pluck. Spirit and courage. Force of character. Attitude."

Women's Wellness [def]:
"All the physical, emotional, spiritual and social aspects of a woman's life. Everything a woman does to achieve and maintain the health she wants. To lead life on her terms. To be happy."

When the vision for this book's topic came to me, I wanted to weave wellness and healthy aging together. But how did I convey the importance of mindset? How does a woman experience wellness in the truest sense of the word if she doesn't address all the whole-istic layers? That's when the word "moxie" popped into my head. It conveys an attitude of true spirit and freedom, which I wanted to invite more women to embrace.

Then, just a few weeks later, I found myself being unexpectedly and magically proposed to on top of the world.

Coincidence?

I would never have attracted the man of my dreams – someone who is also my best friend and supports me 110% – if I hadn't developed some balanced wellness and wholeness first. And I would never have considered bucking the system with an outrageous first marriage at the age of sixty if I didn't have moxie!

Moxie is the secret sauce that juices things up. It can be subtle or overt, but either way it lets you know who you are and allows you to live out loud with spirit and courage. When you live with moxie, it's doubtful that you'll regret anything you did when it comes time to pass on from this lifetime – it's far more likely you'd have regrets because of the things you did NOT make time to say or do.

The purpose of this sixth book in the Woman Of Worth collaborative series is to invite you to live life on your terms and enjoy self-care in a way that makes sense to you and only you. The stories shared here will encourage you to find your tribe, love them hard, and age with laughter, love, grace and gorgeousness from the inside out. No regrets!

As you read this book, you are in for a magnificent adventure guided by some extraordinary yet ordinary women. The very first chapter dives right into body shaming and how we are hoodwinked into not loving what we've been blessed with. We've all gone there, and it's time to lovingly step into the "body-hate free zone."

"No one has ever impacted me by being beautiful or having a perfect body. It might get my initial attention, but it's never been the reason I remembered them. I'm impacted by people for their kindness, loyalty, patience, generosity, vulnerability, humour, spirit, and attitude. I've never said, 'She changed my

life because she was pretty and skinny.' We spend so much time worrying about the thing that means the least to people."
Author Unknown

The momentum continues to build with a diversity of gritty real-life stories from women who have experienced hormonal nightmares, devastating breakups, bullying, cancer, MS, accidents, depression, and more – yet have moved through adversity into triumph. These women pilot planes, belly dance, burlesque, jump into marathons and onto their Harleys ... literally! They are all ages and range from thin to curvy, from vegans to meat-eaters, from moms to single women, from quiet to outrageous. But the one thing they all have in common is they now live life out loud with more moxie.

There is something for everyone in this book. Wherever you're at right now, these stories will inspire you to push the upper limits of your comfort zone and take the next step into a higher level of joy, purpose, and passion. You are a magnificent Woman Of Worth, and you've got moxie baby!

About Christine Awram

"Chocolate is a vegetable, because it comes from a bean." This is just one of many outrageous statements you'll hear from Christine Awram (while wearing a pink tiara) as she encourages women to question any of their beliefs that limit an empowered, joyful, and successful life.

She's the founder of Woman Of Worth WOW Worldwide and is a dynamic speaker, author, visionary, and philanthropist. Christine radiates vitality with her indomitable spirit and humour. Yet her earlier years began as a teenage runaway who experienced addiction, illness and depression. She inspires others by sharing the specific strategies she used to move from futility to fulfillment, and how she transformed challenges into passion and purpose.

Christine's commitment to the empowered leadership of women resulted in her being honoured with the Outstanding Leadership Award by the Global Women's Summit. She has personally inspired over 10,000 women through her WOW events, has published six #1 bestselling books in the last three years, and believes she is just getting warmed up.

www.aWomanOfWorth.com
Facebook: aWomanOfWorthWOW
LinkedIn: wowchristineawram
Twitter: @womanofworthwow

1

Living My Bold, Audacious Life

by Lorna Ketler

"And I said to my body, softly,
I want to be your friend.'
It took a long breath and replied,
'I've been waiting my whole life for this.'"
Nayyirah Waheed

Living My Bold, Audacious Life

By Lorna Ketler

For as long as I can remember, I knew there had to be more to life. The world felt too small for me. I always longed to be somewhere else doing something more fun, more adventurous, more exciting. We lived at the end of a dead-end road, and I remember getting excited if someone made a wrong turn and a strange car had to turn around in our driveway. What story did these strangers have to tell?

I also remember thinking I was unique and special when I was very young, although it wasn't because anyone told me so. In fact, my family came from a modest Mennonite background, which meant that being or feeling special was not encouraged or celebrated. Still, there was a strong seed of belief within me that I had a voice and a place in this world.

Unfortunately, over time those feelings of challenge,

adventure, and inner confidence slowly but surely diminished as new messages came my way. Then, when I was in my early teens, two major events changed my life. First, my mom was diagnosed with a brain tumour. Then, shortly after she made it through the surgery and treatment, my parents separated and eventually divorced. Our family was split up and my brother moved out with my dad. I was understandably emotional and sensitive. I lost focus and interest in school and had teachers who just didn't get me and questioned my behaviour. Who do you think you are? You're too much, too sensitive. Stop asking questions. Why do you cry so easily?

And then there were those beautiful, glossy magazines filled with ads showing me what I needed to do to be beautiful or accepted. They shouted messages of hiding your "flaws," of dressing yourself in a certain way to be attractive to men, of putting yourself through thirty-day regimes to create a "new you." And I certainly didn't have many role models in my life who showed me that our bodies were to be cherished and loved – my beautiful mom was so ashamed of the way she looked that she often tore herself out of photos. As a result, I thought my beauty and sexuality were what I needed to focus on to get anything of value, and that belief led me on a path to some very poor choices.

I found comfort in food and numbed out any negative feelings by eating and drinking. I started to gain weight as a result, and my confidence diminished. I so clearly remember one starlit night when my boyfriend offered to take me for a paddle in a kayak. I wanted to do it so badly, but I was too afraid that my butt wouldn't fit. (I now know that I would have easily fit and have kayaked many times since.) That's a night and experience I'll never get back, lost to the negative messages I had been bombarded with. But even through all this, there was that niggling kernel of knowledge that I deserved better and more. That being "too much" isn't a bad thing. That showing emotion isn't wrong, and that my body deserved to be loved by me, just as it is, in each moment.

The turning point in my life came when I did a college practicum at the Vancouver Women's Health Collective in my early thirties. There, I witnessed new kinds of conversations – ones that empowered me to think about the value of women, about the diversity of our bodies, and about how all bodies are perfect and beautiful. Hearing these words was thrilling, and I began to rethink all I'd been taught to hate about my body.

During this time, I also learned about eating disorders and body dysmorphia and saw their devastating effects. I saw moms refuse to get in the pool or play with their children because they were afraid of being seen. I learned of children as young as five years old who were too afraid to go into a pool without a t-shirt over their swimsuit because they were ashamed of their body. So much SHAME! I knew that this was wrong and dangerous, and I realized that I could make a difference. I could change those thoughts and encourage others to rethink those nasty negative beliefs and feelings, but that had to start with me. If I could shift my own beliefs, maybe I could help others feel differently about themselves. I started to understand that I and everyone else deserve to take up space and be seen in the world.

Change rarely happens overnight, and it certainly didn't with me. I didn't wake up one morning, look in the mirror, and love every part of my body. But I did start talking to myself differently. I became kinder in how I spoke to and about myself, both internally and outwardly. I spoke differently with my girlfriends, reminding them that they were beautiful, full stop. I learned more about the money-generating marketing machine that was teaching us not to accept what we were blessed with, and I baby-stepped my way toward challenging all of it.

Too much of my life had been wasted on missed opportunities and experiences, so I decided to change that as well. Up until now, I'd been saying that I would get my belly button pierced if I had a flat tummy; I loved this rebellious idea but had convinced myself that it wasn't for me. My body was too fat to celebrate, so I would have to wait for that day when my body was "enough." There was so much waiting for the perfect body, moment, or person. And then, on my thirty-third birthday, I stopped waiting and decided that the time was now. I gathered some friends for moral support, fuelled myself with all the courage I could muster, and got my piercing – not for anyone else in the world to see, but to show myself that I was good enough, and that I was worthy of whatever I wanted to gift myself. And in that moment, I felt beautiful and free.

The next step was to wear a bikini – another thing I'd always wanted to do but felt I couldn't – so off I went to the local swimsuit store. I found lovely swim dresses and tankinis and full cover suits, but there were no bikinis available in my size. And why would there be? After all, bikinis weren't meant to be worn on a larger body. I persevered, though, and found a place that made custom swimsuits. There, I had my first ever bikini made just for me.

These two steps were life changing for me. From that point on, I stopped waiting on the sidelines and started to say "yes" to opportunities and experiences. I joined a dragon boating team. I got in a kayak for the very first time. I went on a weeklong singing retreat and went skinny dipping with a bunch of strangers. I took dance lessons with my guy. I travelled to Paris and walked for hours and hours, exploring everything the city had to offer. So many new adventures awaited, and I was no longer going to deny myself any of them.

This new perspective spilled over into other parts of my life as well. I'd always been a lover of fashion, and I enjoyed creating my own style to reflect my personality. Being plus-sized limited my options, though, as funky, fun, and creative plus-size clothing was almost non-existent in my city. Being on a budget limited my options even more. These challenges sparked a dream of opening my own store, and my cousin and I made this dream come true by opening a plus-size consignment store in October of 2000. We were young, naïve, and scared, but we were also so absolutely sure we were doing the right thing by creating a perfect, safe, celebratory space for women of our size. After two years, Bodacious was carrying only new, beautiful plus-sized fashions in an amazing space. I became the sole owner after ten years, and this year I am celebrating twenty years of Bodacious-ness!

The store wasn't (and isn't) about selling clothes for me, although that is such a thrill as well as being necessary for the business to survive and thrive. What I was most interested in were the conversations I got to have with our customers. Before Bodacious, I had no idea how many women – most of them, in fact – hated or were unhappy with their bodies, or how women perpetuated this negative self-image with each other. So, I created a "body-hate free zone" in the store where conversations about diets and flaws were discouraged and seeing the beauty in each person was the rule. As a result, women started being more tender and gentler with themselves. There was less hate and a little more softness. Sometimes, women would stop a negative statement mid-sentence once they saw the sign declaring, "This is a body-hate free zone." The more these conversations changed, the more empowered I became.

After creating this safe haven, I saw myself as an ambassador of sorts. I wanted to show women that you can live your life even when you're not feeling one hundred percent confident. I started posting pictures on social media of me having adventures in my plus-sized body – jumping off boats in a bikini, kayaking, hiking, all the things I'd been too afraid to do for too long. I didn't always love the photos, but I always loved the experience, and I wanted to share that piece to inspire others to take the risk. I wanted to tell people not to let life pass by out of a fear of looking fat or silly or awkward, and that celebrating our lives and bodies can bring so much joy.

Through this experience, I learned that if I showed myself living my life in my lumpy, bumpy, size eighteen body, then others would see that and not be so afraid of doing scary things like going sleeveless on a hot sunny day, taking a trip, getting into a kayak, or saying yes to a dance. By pushing myself and challenging my own fears around how I might look or feel doing something, I've enjoyed some amazing experiences and inspired others to participate more fully in their own lives and see themselves as perfectly beautiful right now, in this moment.

Since posting those photos, I've come to realize that all sizes and ages of women have been taught not to love and accept their physical bodies. There is a fix for everything, from wrinkles and grey hair to big hips and tummies and any other perceived body "flaw." So, here's a thought: what if we stopped accepting those ideas? What if, even for just a moment, we looked in the mirror and saw the full picture of beauty in front of us? A great place to start is to think about what you see when you look at your bestie. Do you see all the less-than-perfect pieces, or do you see a full, complete, beautiful, loving friend who is valuable and worthy of love and acceptance? Well, guess what? That is also true for YOU! And *that* is what we all deserve to see and feel.

When it is the job of the billion dollar beauty industry to make you feel "less than" in order to sell products, changing how we feel about our bodies is not as easy as saying, "Today I'm going to love and accept myself." So, here are some ideas for how you can dance in the enjoyment of beautiful YOU.

First, think about what fabric feels beautiful on your skin or what item of clothing makes you feel invincible. What puts that little kick in your step? Is it silk? Velvet? Maybe a super lightweight cotton that just whispers over your body? Is it cowboy boots, or maybe some stilettos? Find something in that fabric or that one piece of clothing to add to your collection of items to celebrate you. It doesn't have to cost a fortune; you can go on a fun quest through your local consignment store to find that magic silk scarf, cashmere sweater, or rockstar pair of shoes that make you feel kick-ass. My go-to is always a favourite pair of chunky boots – they make me feel like a superhero.

What I wear and how I feel in my body changes from day to day, and I certainly don't wake up every morning loving every part of me. However, I've wasted enough time being negative about my body, and what I have learned is to not *hate* parts of me. Sometimes, neutrality is the bigger goal. To help achieve this, try gently sending love and acceptance to a part of your body that you normally criticize.

As you go out in the world to find the clothes that make you feel invincible, make sure you are looking in stores that feel safe and celebratory. I've heard too many nightmarish stories about women who have been treated terribly when looking for clothes that fit their body. Negative messaging does not belong anywhere in retail – or anywhere at all, for that matter. Call ahead, if that makes you more comfortable, so you can ask about what sizes, styles, and support are available. Ask for help, and if you don't get it, go somewhere else. Get recommendations from friends and family for places that will fit your needs and desires and welcome you in. And when you do find that store, let go of the size on the label. After twenty years in the industry, I can tell you that one label's extra large is another's size eight. You just have to try things on and not let the size define you.

Next, break the flippin' rules! Screw the idea of "What Not to Wear" – clothes don't have to be flattering and slimming. Make your own personal statement and wear it with pride. Love orange? Wear it! Love horizontal stripes? I double dare you! It's your body and your rules, and quite frankly, what you wear is nobody else's business. My biggest fashion faux pas is my oversized khaki overalls – they're NOT traditionally flattering by any means, but they are fun and silly and they make me happy.

If you're shopping with a friend, tell her she's beautiful no matter what. I've seen souls crushed outside of the dressing room by mothers, friends, and spouses. Pay attention to what lights your friend up and help her see it. Do her eyes light up? Does she twirl or dance as she exits the dressing room? That's magic, right there!

I've also found it helpful to find style icons who can give you ideas on new ways to embrace your style. One of my icons is Iris Apfel – if you've never heard of her, I highly suggest looking up this ninety-eight-year-old rule breaker and fashion inspiration. Another is the Accidental Icon. As my hair gets grayer and my body shifts into new ways of being, my inspirations have shifted to match – they all are in the fifty-plus category. Representation really does matter. Seeing women living their lives fully encourages me to live in the moment without fear or doubt, and watching others break the rules encourages me to step up and out.

However, maybe for you it's not about fashion at all. Maybe what will light you up is wearing your favourite hiking boots on a walk in the forest. I did a 100-kilometre pilgrimage in Spain for my fiftieth birthday, and putting my boots and backpack on each morning felt so freeing. Those boots grounded me and made me feel invincible! Well, almost – there were some really big hills to climb. Or, maybe it's letting the water touch your skin. The biggest reason I chose to start wearing a two-piece swimsuit is because I LOVE the feel of the water on my skin, and swimsuits always got in the way of that. If I could skinny dip anywhere and everywhere, I would! If anyone is worried about how I look in my bikini, that's their problem, not mine.

Finally, work on loving your body exactly as it is now. Write down twenty things you love about yourself, such as a body part or a characteristic, and post that list on your mirror or bulletin board so you can reflect on it each morning. Then, go out in the world and let yourself have fun! Dance, play, twirl, whatever feels good in that moment.

My heart is full from the stories that have been shared with me over the past twenty years – stories from women who have had terrible experiences in other stores, or had finally taken a fashion risk that they were afraid of, or had just finally found a safe and soft place to land. We all deserve to be treated with love and respect, both at home and out in the world, and it's something our world needs more of right now. So get out there, spread a bit of love and kindness, and see the beauty in everyone – starting with yourself. Be bodacious and audacious and celebrate your uniqueness every day.

About Lorna Ketler

Lorna Ketler is the owner and lead body-love enthusiast at Bodacious Lifestyles Inc, a women's clothing store that offers a fun, safe, welcoming environment where all bodies are beautiful and worthy of being celebrated. Her store is located in Victoria, BC, but can also be found online and at various pop-up shops throughout the lower mainland. Through her store, and through her online presence, she passionately encourages women to fully recognize and appreciate their beauty, their bodies, and their curves.

Lorna delights in seeing the world from a fresh perspective. As she approached fifty, she decided that she would create an "epic" experience each month over the course of a year, starting with walking one hundred kilometres of the Camino de Santiago on her fiftieth birthday. She then filled her months with big and small experiences including jewelry making classes, painting workshops, travel, and most importantly, spending precious time with dear friends.

Celebrating twenty years in business this year, Lorna plans to enjoy that accomplishment by exploring new adventures and opportunities, including making art and having a big, bodacious dance party! After five years of living on her boat, Lorna now enjoys living in beautiful Victoria, BC, with her husband and best friend George.

www.bodacious.ca

2

Cross That Finish Line and Liberate Your Inner Champion

by Gail Thevarge

"New beginnings are often disguised as painful endings."
Lao Tzu

Cross That Finish Line and Liberate Your Inner Champion

By Gail Thevarge

I may not look like an athlete, but at fifty-eight years of age, I can proudly say that I am an international runner. How did I go from the depths of despair to crossing finish lines throughout Western Canada and the US? I set a goal, did the work, and crossed the finish line. In the process, I have received so many additional benefits – ones that I could never have imagined when I first started running, but that I now cannot imagine living without. By sharing my story, I hope to show you how completing goals that seem so distant can give you a feeling of intense accomplishment, reawaken long-lost confidence, and reignite your desires.

In my previous life (before marriage and children), I worked in downtown Vancouver. I started as a file clerk in the regional office of a bank, then became a teller, and then moved into a career in mortgages at various trust companies. I took courses in my free time, which was the beginning of my lifelong journey of learning. I was happy and independent, and I usually had a positive outlook on life. Like most women at that time, I started doing Jane Fonda exercise videos in my living room before advancing to aerobics classes in a gym, complete with headbands and leg warmers. Not only did I want look like I was in shape, but I also had a vision of myself being a fit, healthy, vibrant senior in the future. I felt strong and in control.

Then came marriage, children, and a move to the Okanagan. I loved being a mother and wife – my children meant the world to me, and I enjoyed every moment spent with them. My focus was on being the best parent I could be, which meant my fitness took a backseat to these responsibilities. Gym workouts were replaced with chasing children around a playground, although I did go to some Pilates and yoga classes when I could.

Unfortunately, when my kids were nine and eleven years old, things came crashing down and I became a separated, single parent. I was devastated and completely unprepared. The next year was a blur. My children needed their mother to be fully functioning and present for them, but I was barely existing. Every morning I woke up hoping that it had just been a nightmare, that my old life would be waiting for me when I opened my eyes, but it never was. So, I got up, put on a smile, and tried to be brave for my children. I was lost and confused, aimlessly stumbling through each day, desperately wanting to be the person I was before. I also wanted to be a great role model for my children, and I knew that who I was right now wasn't it.

I needed a change – a big one that would give me a purpose and a mission. I needed a goal so far out of my comfort zone that completing it would pull that confident person back out from inside of me.

One day, I remembered a conversation I'd had with my stepdaughter Chantel a few years before. She had phoned me after completing her first Vancouver Sun Run – a ten-kilometre run around downtown Vancouver – and I had been able to feel her excitement through the phone. She had ecstatically recounted how she had been called an athlete at the end of the run and told me that it was her greatest memory of the day. Her enthusiasm during that call stayed with me, and as I thought back on it from this place of despair, I realized that this was the kind of goal I needed – something that would be demanding but also rewarding. I wanted to feel that type of excitement and enthusiasm for life again. And with that, I became a runner.

My first challenge was a 5.4-kilometre run through my community, which took place as part of the annual Action Fest weekend festival. My eleven-year-old son also accepted the challenge and signed up, but since he was already active in school and other activities, he didn't require the additional preparation that I did. I started training on my own, one step at a time. Sometimes I trained on a treadmill at the recreation centre, other times outside in my neighbourhood. I had no idea what an actual running event would be like, so I just ran. At times, during these early days of training, I had a glimpse of what it was like to feel free. When I was pushing myself physically, the things that concerned me seemed to be just a little bit smaller. When I finished a training session, I would have a sense of pride for completing the training, and I would feel a little lighter.

When the big day arrived, I was scared, excited, and committed to completing the run. Before the race began, the fitness instructors from the recreation centre lead us through a warmup – perhaps I was an athlete already! Then, we were off. The day was hot and the course seemed to stretch on forever. Thankfully, some caring homeowners put on their sprinklers so the participants could run through them to cool off, and volunteers were handing out water to the runners at aid stations throughout the course. Other volunteers held signs to stop traffic in order to keep the runners safe, and all of the volunteers cheered and provided encouragement. Some congratulated me for taking on the challenge. At no time during the event did I feel like quitting; I just kept picturing myself running across the finish line. Completing the run would provide such a sense of accomplishment while quitting would lead me even further into despair, and that was not an option. That day, when I crossed the finish line with so many people cheering for me, I felt like an athlete. I felt stronger than I had in months, and I was proud of myself for taking on this challenge and completing it.

I did this same run each June for the next few years, with both my son and daughter joining me after that first run. I always looked forward to the event, and every year I worked on finishing faster than the time before. Eventually, though, I began looking for new challenges. I came across a program to train for the Vancouver Sun Run. It was ten kilometres, but I figured that since I was already doing five, I could surely do ten with training. I signed up, and my daughter joined me.

After thirteen weeks of training with a fantastic group of leaders and participants, we were off to Vancouver. Standing at the start line with more than 55,000 people was an experience unlike any other. There is an excitement that comes from being with people of all ages and ability levels, all sharing a common goal to cross the finish line no matter what. As we made our way along the route, there were bands playing, people cheering us on with signs boasting humorous slogans, and beautiful scenery to take in.

At the last ramp, near the end of the run, former Olympic athlete and medalist Lynn Kanuka (Williams) cheered the runners on. She had been a speaker at one of our training sessions, and her story of winning a medal for Canada was inspiring. It has been many years since she brought home the bronze medal, but she still looked amazing. Nowadays she travels throughout BC inspiring people to train for and complete the Sun Run through the SportMedBC InTraining Program. And now here she was, cheering me and my fellow runners on.

The run was hard, but I kept telling myself that each step that I took was one step closer to the finish line. I kept saying I would feel so incredible crossing that finish line, and I was right.

After two years of running in the Sun Run, I was fortunate to become a leader with the Penticton InTraining Program. For the past three years, I have encouraged many runners each Saturday morning through the thirteen-week training program. It has truly been a gift to be able to inspire new runners and show them that they can complete the run if they simply trust the program.

After a few more years of training for and participating in the Sun Run, I came across an advertisement for a run through Disneyland. As a huge Disneyland fan, I thought that running in the park would be a dream come true. I was further motivated by the realization that all finishers would receive a spectacular finisher's medal – it turns out that I am completely motivated by t-shirts and medals. Also, the Disney run happened shortly after the Sun Run, so my daughter and I would already be trained and ready to go.

As we stood in our corral at four in the morning on the day

of the race, waiting for the sun to rise and our turn to start, the excitement was incredible. This time, I motivated myself with a reminder that the most amazing Tinker Bell medal would be mine at the finish line. The American anthem was sung, and then it was time to start.

The run was an incredible experience. After many years of going to Disneyland, I thought I was very familiar with the park and all it had to offer. However, the course took us through some behind-the-scenes locations and brought us into the park at different places than I was used to. I was fortunate to be able to share this experience with my teenage daughter – at a time when many teenagers do not want to spend time with their mothers, having my daughter travel with me and share in this achievement was yet another benefit. This was also the first time she finished a run ahead of me, and she will never let me forget it.

Once I got involved in running, more and more events started appearing – they must have always been out there in the abyss, but now they were calling me. My former dragon boat coach Lynn told a fellow paddler and I about many of the runs she had done over the years, and on her advice, my daughter, our international student, and I signed up for and completed the ten-kilometre run in Ucluelet, British Columbia. This was a difficult run with many hills, but the scenery was well worth the "extreme" effort. The trails wound through the most amazing evergreen trees before emerging high on the top of the cliffs overlooking the beautiful blue ocean, with white-capped waves crashing on the rocks below. At times like this, I feel so grateful that I can participate in this sport in such beautiful venues.

Another event that Lynn brought to our attention was the Rock and Roll Marathon in Vegas. My friend Alynda did some research and found that if you ran two events during the weekend, you receive three medals, two shirts, and free beer at the finish line. There was a five-kilometre warm up run on Saturday night, then a ten-kilometre run, half marathon, and full marathon the next night. We opted for the ten-kilometre distance. Running down the strip at night with the excitement, the lights, the music, and the thousands of other runners made for an unforgettable experience, especially since this is the only time the strip is closed to traffic. And, travelling and running with my daughter and friend made for an amazing weekend.

At the start of each year, I have been setting a new goal for the runs I want to accomplish. For 2019, my goal was to do five runs, and for one of them to be a half marathon. To achieve the latter part of this goal, Lynn, Alynda and I travelled to Couer D'Alene in Idaho for an event that took place over the Memorial Day long weekend. I was concerned that I hadn't trained enough to be able to complete the half marathon, but I reminded myself that I wasn't competing against anyone. I just had to take it one step at a time, one kilometre at a time, and get to the finish line however I could. Alynda, who chose to do the ten-kilometre run instead, ran the final portion of the race with me and provided encouragement to help me cross the finish line. The finisher medal and shirt from that race are two of my most prized possessions, and spending the weekend with friends in a new destination made for even more amazing memories.

For 2020, my goal is again to complete five races, but this time two of them will be half marathons. There are so many options to choose from: a run from Oregon to Washington across the Bridge of the Gods; Beat the Blurch in Carnation, Washington, where they provide birthday cake and Nutella sandwiches at the water stations; and even a run in the Cowichan Valley which includes wine tasting and a catered dinner. I already know I will be joining the Beer for Breakfast team for the annual beer run in Penticton in June.

Running is now an integral part of my life, and the rewards I have received are significant in ways I could never have imagined. Every time I complete a new challenge, I feel stronger. I know that I can do whatever I set my mind to do, and when I complete the goals I set for myself, I create a feeling of power and confidence which is directly transferable to my work, relationships, and everything I do. Running also creates energy, both physically and mentally, that reaches all aspects of my life. I am now even better, stronger and more confident than I was in my "previous life" before marriage and children.

Another unexpected benefit of running is the friendships that I have either made or grown substantially through running and the fun we've had along the way. Travelling and sharing these events and adventures with close friends has made this journey even more enjoyable, and having friends to train with has made me more accountable for showing up to the regular training runs.

When it comes to setting goals, as a wise person once said, "begin with the end in mind." For me, that end was a picture of what kind of senior I wanted to be. I do not want to be dependent on medication for health issues that are within my control to prevent. I do not want to be someone who lives in constant pain from sore and stiff joints. I do not want to have to take endless medications every day and live a lackluster life. In my world, seventy and beyond is the new fifty, and at seventy I want to be running marathons, discovering new adventures, and crushing every goal. Although I cannot see into the future or completely control how my life will unfold, I want to do as much as I can each day to become the person I want to be. I'm not fast, I'm not consistent, and I do let life get in the way. But

I always cross the finish line, and I feel better than I have in years, both mentally and physically. I am always registered for the next race because not having an event on the horizon is not an option for me. I visualize myself hanging the next medal on my special medal rack that I brought back from Las Vegas, wearing the next shirt, and connecting intimately with the next destination.

If you are ready to unlock the greatness that you may have lost, find a huge goal – one that scares the daylights out of you – and commit to it. Sign up, bring your friends, and take just one step towards your goal, and then another. When the training starts, be there on time and ready to go. Take it all in. Let the leader or trainer inspire you. Find something in their story that you can relate to and use it to get you going when you don't feel like showing up.

Also, remember that you're not "too old." There are runners in all age categories and ability levels, and there are destinations around the corner as well as all over the world. Or, if running isn't your thing, try hiking, or weightlifting, or cycling, or any number of activities. Find what calls to you and just go for it.

No matter what your goal, how you cross the finish line isn't important. It doesn't have to be pretty, and it usually isn't. All that matters is that you do it. Just put one foot in front of the other and liberate your inner champion.

About Gail Thevarge

Gail's mantra is "whatever it takes," and she uses this to complete challenges in all areas of her life. Her vision is to inspire other women to reignite their desires by completing large goals, to be an example that it's never too late to start something new, and to constantly push past self-imposed limits to reach new heights that were previously unimaginable. Being an author in this book is another example of a larger-than-life challenge that Gail felt compelled to conquer – one that was unlike anything she has done previously and was so far out of her comfort zone.

Gail's greatest passion is to travel, and she is at her best when she is able to combine runs with travelling to new destinations each year. She resides in Summerland in the beautiful Okanagan Valley and loves spending time with her two amazing children, Taylor and Emily, while awaiting the next big challenge and adventure.

Email: egt_home@shaw.ca
Instagram: @gailthevarge3

3

Claiming My Truths – Moxie, Mayhem, and Magic

by Ange Frymire, RTC, MBA

*"What the caterpillar calls the end of the world,
the master calls a butterfly."*
Richard Bach

Claiming My Truths – Moxie, Mayhem, and Magic

By Ange Frymire, RTC, MBA

There's a popular saying for those who "live young," and it's one that I'm owning today: "I'm sixty-four going on forty." That's me! I'm aging gracefully, feeling much younger than I am, and living a fulfilling, blessed life in so many ways. Adult successes have been numerous over these past three decades, but none of them would have been possible without the boulders that I had to climb to see the rainbows on the other side.

Born on April Fool's Day, I was often the brunt of sometimes cruel family jokes on my birthday, such as receiving massive boxes which I unwrapped each year with gusto – our family was poor, so presents were manna from heaven. At the bottom of these packages might be a pair of salt-and-pepper shakers, my brothers' dirty socks, or male underwear with holes in them.

The family usually howled at my shock and dismay; I laughed with them, embarrassing as it was, but I felt as worthless as the underwear. Such pranks pushed me further into my own world. I was a shy one growing up and often stayed in the background. I was quiet around visitors and friends as I had no idea what to say or do, so they didn't often play with me. This added to my belief that no one really cared about me, and that there was something wrong with me.

These limiting perceptions were further fuelled by living in a chaotic family with seven other siblings and an often-absent father who flew across the world on military missions. My mother was emotionally vacant much of the time; she was sickly, angry, and alone. Depression had clamped onto her like an excavator grips a boulder. Her inability to manage the household drove her deeper into the abyss, creating a bed-ridden, overwhelmed person who struggled with her marriage, children, and neighbours.

Today, I know how much she loved her children during her eighty-seven years of living. I also know that her own tortuous childhood left her in a place where she didn't know how to love herself.

I made peace with my father when I was forty-four and found my mother's true loving self when I turned fifty. Forgiving and surrendering a childhood that had borne many scars has opened up a vista of endless possibilities in loving Mom and Dad fully and completely, both then and posthumously. I'm so grateful to have had parents who did the best that they could with the tools they'd picked up along their own life journeys.

As I have grown, I've found that there's something special about claiming April Fool's Day as my birthday. It's the first sign of the zodiac and the first day of the month. My birthday also created another first in the family: I was almost born on the living room floor on the airbase in Winnipeg, a story my mother often told in my early years.

People remember my birthday because of what the day offers: laughter, jokes, and gaiety. Although I despised the painful stunts that were played on others, the pranks helped me realize a truth: people *did* care about me. Eventually, I was able to laugh at some of the jokes and looked forward to that special day, even planning my adult parties six weeks in advance. It was the beginning of one of several transformations in my life, and I began to emerge from my cocoon.

Although my birthday was the start of my journey, there is one period of my life that stands out as the ultimate game-changer. It began when my husband had his first of several breakdowns in 2016. We'd met when I was fifty and married five years later. It was a first marriage for both of us, and I was so in love with this man. In our seventh year of marriage – one that was both rocky and filled with joy – we enrolled in a workshop that brought me to my next journey. Seven of us at this workshop bonded and enrolled in a three-year transpersonal experiential program that trained students as therapeutic counsellors. I saw it as a complement to my job teaching at the university, a career that I'd embraced for the past twenty-one years.

My husband's first breakdown came six days after the program had started, and he would go on to have seven more over the next year. My heart burst open day after day as I stood powerless to do anything to stop his declining mental health, his growing self-loathing, his fear of people, and his isolation from friends and neighbours. In three years, his severe withdrawal from the marriage included detaching from physical affection and spousal intimacy as well as long bouts of silence. The doctor's diagnosis scared the living daylights out of me: acute anxiety and chronic depression or dysthymia, also known as double depression. His condition is also known as diffuse physiological arousal. This condition increases one's heart rate and blood pressure while decreasing frontal lobe activity, thereby impairing judgment, decision-making, and the ability to listen and empathize.

I went into overdrive with teaching, continuing my course work, volunteering, and taking care of him, which brought me smack into overwhelm. Over the next year, I fell apart in two of my classes, crying and leaving the campus in humiliation and shame. I quit all volunteer work. My husband's emotional health worsened, as did my own reactions to the heartbreak and devastation of watching him retreat further and further away. Fifteen months later, my doctor named what was happening with me as well.

Depression.

This diagnosis gripped me so deeply that I was unable to cope, bursting into tears several times a day. I flatly refused to accept his conclusion, which brought me to my emotional knees time and time again. I remember taking the dean of the School of Business out for lunch to thank her for all she'd done for me since my husband's first breakdown, and when she asked how my husband was doing, I broke down in tears in the restaurant. The shame that floated to the surface seemed insurmountable. I finally went on disability leave and endured eight months of hell. The depression was drowning me in despair. It was inconceivable. Impossible. I seemed to inherit spiritual agony when even thinking about "depression."

While the diagnosis caught me off guard, today I see that this condition had been present for a long time. I also recognized the addictive behaviours I'd adopted to banish it, from people-pleasing to workaholism to overeating.

Depression runs in my family, so it's not surprising that the gene lives within me.

As the days grew longer, this gaping hole of grief was buried so deep that I couldn't get out of bed. After more than two months of crying from five to fifteen hours a day, I felt whipped. I still couldn't accept that I was depressed as naming it meant owning it. However, being unable to name my captor meant being unable to tame it. Treating it also came with its own set of barriers. The thought of pursuing therapy added more shame as we'd already seen four marriage counsellors, and now I needed my own therapist. My doctor had also prescribed me antidepressants six months earlier, but I'd consistently refused to take them, having seen how they'd mixed up Mom throughout her life and my husband over the past two years.

The tears increased, the desperation surged, and the isolation mushroomed. The only salvation I could cling to was my circle of mighty companions in my therapy counselling program. Had I not been in those classes, I may have fallen into that abyss my mother had lived in most of her life.

When my father died in September of 2018, my life spiralled deeper into the pits of grief, desolation, and hopelessness. I felt like an avalanche tearing down the mountainside with its boulders crushing my spirit, my joy, my marriage, and my life as I'd known it.

Everything changed in the early morning of December 4, 2018. I'd been awake since 3:00 a.m., unable to calm myself down. I can still feel the scattered thoughts that had jumped in bed with me the night before; my mind said I was unlovable, that my husband couldn't emotionally support me, that he didn't care, and that I was so alone. Thought after senseless thought tumbled through my pyjamas and planted themselves in my prefrontal cortex. I was sinking in a sea of damaged neurotransmitters that jolted my shield of safety, plummeting me into suicidal ideation. It took me over thirty minutes to realize I'd been thinking that it wasn't worth living anymore. What the fuck was going on? I LOVED life, even when it was hard, so how the hell could I even THINK of suicide? I was going to live to be over one hundred, dammit! Who was this dangerous stalker destroying my life?

The shock and horror of that moment were so great that I grabbed my cell phone and posted "help help help" on my WhatsApp thread with my class of nineteen other counselling peers. Within a few minutes, five had called to talk with me. One mighty companion stayed on the phone with me for over an hour in the evening to just listen and be there emotionally while I, barely talking, wept endlessly. I was in disbelief that I'd just been thinking of suicide and felt as though I'd been locked in a jail cell with no doors or windows. Even though it was so difficult to accept my depression, the truth was branded into my psyche.

The next day, another sleepless night brought me yet again to morning insanity. It was almost as though the emotional script written the day before was being continued and emphasized. I began imagining what I'd say in the note I'd write to my husband, family, and friends about why I'd committed suicide. It took me another long, painstakingly slow thirty minutes to register that I'd once again been imprisoned by suicidal ideation. I reached out again, and my friends stayed on the line to talk me down from my emotional crisis. These "dark nights of the soul" were terrifying.

When I was finally able to get up that morning, I walked to my dresser and stared at that unopened package of tiny pink pain-poppers, with its promise to crystalize depression and ban it forever. I pushed open the thin foil protector and held the pill in my hand for at least a minute. "Take a deep breath, Ange," I said to myself. "You NEED this." Then, after sixty-four years of sad-and-beautiful, chaotic-and-blessed living – mixed with moxie, mayhem, and magic – I took my first antidepressant.

It's fitting to use the euphemism that December 5, 2018 was another first day of the rest of my life. (It happens with me still; I live with a handful of "firsts.") I stayed on antidepressants for about three months and then weaned myself off under the watchful yet disagreeing eye of my physician. I continued to seek personal and couples' therapy. As the marital fights increased, our home screamed this ghostly silence of a marriage collapsing while the synapses of connections were ripped from their resting place. My journal now birthed more vulnerable, biting writing of my inner wars and wins. Writing – one of my healing tools – released some of the talons of depression. I focused intensely on my therapy course, which helped me to see both myself and my husband in those pages of weary words. I visited the doctor weekly for months, saw my therapist monthly, and began to recover from the minefield of unstable mental health.

It was with great sadness that I eventually realized a truth about my husband: he simply could not register or decipher what was happening within me, and he couldn't support me in my fall from grace. He once said he was angry that I was depressed because I was supposed to support *him* in his own mire. I was flabbergasted when he first said this. Now, however, I feel such sadness for his own sense of being abandoned by his wife because of her own depression. It was so difficult for him to see that the crumbling marriage had fueled my own loss of identity.

During one particularly raging fight with him after he'd broken a serious promise about drinking and driving, I drove and argued with him in the car about broken promises, betrayal, lying, and responsibility. The feelings of betrayal were old. My wiser self knew they weren't real as his behaviour was one of the sidebars of his increasing mental collapse, but I was still angry. After thirty minutes of arguing, he finally asked me to "stop raging" at him. I was shocked! I *had* been raging at him, just as my parents had done with each other throughout their thirty years of marriage. I was also in awe that he had spoken up; over the last seven years, he'd often just lapsed into what appeared to be stone-cold silence.

I stayed quiet for the rest of the drive home while my body, mind, and spirit leapt into acute awareness. In raging with him, in reviewing all of those fights, in wanting his physical affection so badly that I felt as though I was living alone, I could feel the strong pull of depression luring me, tempting me, sweet-talking me to join it. It whispered that I didn't have to do anything because it would take care of everything. IT was my salvation. IT would save me. That voice was so powerful that I could feel its grip tugging on me, pulling me down, down, down.

Suddenly, in a split second of earth-shattering insight, I saw how easy it could be to return to that place of darkness away from a world that is cold, unknown, and unsafe. A place where depression is the blanket that keeps you covered up, protects you from pain, and prevents others from hurting you.

I saw this through the lens of my mother's eye – how she had let it in, and how it took over eighty years to leave her. It petrified me, just as much as those two instances of suicidal ideation had.

When we arrived home, blood pulsed through my body. We walked into the house and to our bedroom in silence. I sat on a chair and watched him climb into bed. Then, I listened to the quiet, calm voice inside that knew what needed to be done.

The words of Ralph Waldo Emerson came to mind: "What you are afraid to do is a clear indication of the next thing you need to do." I ended the relationship before I went to bed – a relationship which was broken, damaged, and irreparable.

When I awoke the next morning, I felt light. Cleansed. It was as though I'd shed a 500-pound weight from my body. I felt it in my walk, my talk, my smile, and my psyche.

Today, I'm single and feel more alive than I've felt in years. It's not because I left my husband or gave up on the marriage, even though there is some truth in that. It's because for the first time in this intimate relationship, I'd said "yes" to me. I'd said "no" to depression.

There are times when I regret the years of living without honouring myself. When I fall into that trap, I meet my angry self who couldn't "save" the marriage. It's at those critical times that I have to take a step back and repair my thinking.

I couldn't have done this without therapy, my friends, some incredibly supportive family members, and my cats, who are two of the most supportive souls in the world. Each of those supports were instrumental in my ability to be willing and ready; to step in, stay in, and look around without judgement (which was often hard) and with surrender (which became easier). Eventually, I found my way in the world again.

Fellow counselling students, teachers, and grads helped me work through the pits of my fears each week over the three years I was in the therapy program. I also benefitted from writing down the scattered thoughts of my fears of the crumbling marriage, and of the childhood wounds from abuse, abandonment, and guilt that greeted me upon many sunrises. In response to these writings, the teachers, classmates, and grads posted support and asked questions about my family-of-origin issues that brought me deeper into the vortex of vulnerability.

They helped me see many truths about who I was in all of this, where I could make choices, and how to embrace these parts of my disowned self. My personal struggle really mattered to them, and they helped me see how to matter to myself first.

The organization I studied under – Clearmind International – taught me how important connection is, and how seeing the world through the eyes of love can help rewrite our stories. The learnings of therapeutic counselling taught me to see my clients in a completely different light. It helped me to see how we can claim ourselves when we come into the therapy room feeling broken, damaged, and doomed. I've also returned to teaching at the university, a career in which I've found so much joy and passion. Even when I retire, I'll always be a teacher; this is what my passion has helped me claim.

As I continued to heal, I found the strength to see my husband's light, to live in my own light, and to allow us both to move at our own pace. We are no longer together, but he is still my friend. We tried being roommates, intent on establishing a platonic friendship, but I need more time on my own first. I want to do this relationship with him differently so that I remember how it feels to see him – and me – through the non-judgemental eyes of compassion.

I've been writing from my soul, compiling a novel and writing memoirs. My writing itch has been taking me deeper into my family secrets and out to the other side of the mountain. It's a sacred chalice of love, compassion, authenticity, and integrity, sprinkled with some pinches of self-doubt, some periods of not feeling worthy enough, and the wisdom to know that these feelings are simply not true. They're my signposts, standing tall when I need to go back inside to reflect, reframe, and integrate.

I have many tools in my wellness kit as I hit the age of retirement – my seventh career in a life I now know is blessed.

My spiritual practice is morning yoga and meditation. For almost two decades, I've been saying gratitude prayers when I go to bed; they help me connect to my compassion for family, friends, and my ex-husband, helping me to stay in integrity and congruency. I'm not perfect, which I still sometimes aim for, and which my friends lovingly remind me gets in the way of my ability to live in peace. I'm taking care of me; I'm staying true to who am I and who I'm not. I still find peace in the shadows and light in the dark.

And this I know: I'm still in the dark at times. But it's different now, because I climb out by changing my thoughts and opening my eyes.

About Ange Frymire

Ange Frymire leads an active, passionate life as teacher, writer, facilitator, mentor, life coach, communicator, and therapeutic counsellor. She founded a boutique communications firm in 1992 and began teaching in 1995, which mushroomed into teaching business writing to university students. She was a co-author of *Fundamentals of Public Relations and Marketing Communications in Canada* and has had numerous stories and articles published. She is also a best-selling author through participating in her first collaborative book, *Family Tree: Embracing Your Mother Daughter Roots for Forgiveness, Fulfillment and Freedom.* Her debut novel will be launched in 2020.

Continuous studying of the human psyche and behaviours has led Ange to thirty years of senior-level business expertise in communications, social responsibility, employee engagement, media relations, and stakeholder development. After her husband became ill, she focused on her studies in psychodynamic therapeutic counselling with Clearmind International and is now a licensed, registered therapeutic counsellor.

Ange is a tireless volunteer for boards and committees who specialize in the humanity of society. This passion has rewarded her with the "Canadian Mentor of the Year" award by the Canadian Public Relations Society, as well as being named a fellow with its College of Fellows. She is also president of the Association of Cooperative Counselling Therapists of Canada.

Email: vocalpoint@telus.net

4

Turning My Curse Into My Blessing

by Jennifer Desloges

"There is no greater agony than bearing an untold story inside you."
Maya Angelou

Turning My Curse Into My Blessing

By Jennifer Desloges

Sometimes, we face problems in our lives that seem almost impossible to overcome. They consume our thoughts, change the way we feel about ourselves, and stop us from stepping into who we are truly meant to be. These problems can feel like a curse that is impossible to shake, but I am here to tell you that you can take that curse and turn it into a blessing that will change your life for the better.

My "curse" first made an appearance when I started growing a full beard and male-type body hair at the age of nineteen. I was afraid to do anything about it at first, having heard that shaving makes the hair come back thicker, so I just left it there. Eventually, I gathered up enough courage to ask my doctor what to do. He didn't ask me any questions or order any tests; he just told me to shave it. I was shocked by his lack of tact, and by his seemingly thoughtless advice. In my opinion, men shaved their faces, not women. I began spending twenty to thirty minutes every weekday and three to four hours every Saturday and Sunday tweezing. This just wasn't enough to stay ahead of the problem, so I had to resort to shaving by Thursday each week. Little did I know that my doctor had actually given me good advice. In 1928, Dr. Mildred Trotter proved that shaving does not affect hair growth. Yes, the hair feels blunt and seems thicker, but when the shaved hairs shed and fall out, the new hairs are exactly the same as the ones from before shaving. In contrast, tweezing makes the hairs stronger, deeper, and bigger because of increased blood flow (the food for the hair). If only this doctor had spent some time and explained this to me – if only he had shown some compassion and cared – then he could have saved me considerable time and pain.

For the next eight years, I struggled to hide my problem. My days were filled with obsessive tweezing routines and paranoia. If I was talking to someone and their eyes shifted to my chin, I would start sweating and want to hide. I always covered my face with my hands – a nervous habit that has persisted to this day. It got to the point that I didn't want to leave my home or be in the company of others, tormented by my feelings of shame and frustration. I even questioned my gender as I had developed some other male traits, including aggression and anger issues. I thought of myself as being the bearded lady, since that was the only human I could relate too.

Throughout this time, I never discussed my hair problem with anyone – not even my husband. We had gotten married when I was seventeen, before my hair problem began, and I had gone to great lengths to hide it from him. I didn't want him to know, although in retrospect he must have known to some degree. After all, he was never allowed to touch my face, and he did walk in on a few of my tweezing marathons. For many years, we both just pretended the hair wasn't there.

Unbeknownst to me, my hair problems were tied into other health issues as well. When my husband and I decided to grow our family, we struggled with some fertility problems. We conceived four times, but I lost two and went into early labour with the others. Thankfully we were able to have two wonderful children, but my hair problem got worse with each pregnancy. I tried electrolysis in 1984 after my daughter was born, but my face broke out so bad that it looked like ground beef. I also wasn't seeing results as the hair was still coming back. I now know that this was not right, and that the electrologist was not doing a good job. I quit electrolysis when I got pregnant with my son out of fear that it would make me miscarry again, and even though that fear ended up being unfounded, I'm glad that I did. I feel if I had continued with the treatment, I would have ended up with permanent scars and nerve damage.

It wasn't until I was twenty-seven years old that I was diagnosed with polycystic ovarian syndrome (PCOS) after developing extremely painful fibroids in my womb. PCOS is a disorder in which a woman's hormones become out of balance, causing a variety of symptoms such as excess body and facial hair, mood swings, irregular or absent menstruation, weight problems, hair loss, painful intercourse, long term or severe acne, high blood pressure, skin discolouration, and skin tags. I was very lucky that I got married young and started a family early as many women with PCOS have trouble conceiving and carrying to term – myself included. My doctor encouraged me to have a hysterectomy, but at the time I wasn't ready to give up the possibility of having more children. However, the pain I was experiencing increased during menstruation and continued to worsen over time. By 1990, my period was so bad that I took just about everything I could get my hands on. I even tried to take tranquilizers that had been prescribed to my husband, but when I went to get them, I found him standing in front of the medicine chest. He said, "You have two choices: go to bed and wait for the pain to pass or go to the hospital and tell them what you've already taken, because you're not getting anything else tonight." I went to bed.

A few days later, my husband told me that it was time to get the hysterectomy; he couldn't watch me suffer anymore. I called the surgeon's office and asked for possible surgery dates, and I was told they were booking three months out. So, I scheduled an appointment for a consultation and went in. When I told the doctor that I was ready, he left the room and came back with my surgery date: Tuesday. He said he didn't want to wait. I was shocked and cried all the way home, but I still went through with it. During the surgery, the doctor discovered that my ovaries were covered with cysts – he had to remove one entirely and took out about half of the remaining one.

In the years leading up to my hysterectomy, I continued to struggle with my hair problem. I felt like I was cursed. I had an amazing husband, beautiful children, and all this happiness around me, but I couldn't shake the deep unhappiness that lived inside of me. I felt so ugly and dirty all the time. Every minute of my life was controlled by my hair situation – I always had to be on guard, ensuring I didn't forget and embarrass myself. As a result, I had become a difficult person to live with. Even as young infants, my children knew to never touch my face. I would reinforce sternly, "Never touch mommy's face." I would also panic every time my husband touched me. I remember one time when I curled up behind him in bed and hugged his back, and he said, "Oh, what did you poke me with?" It was whiskers from shaving. I was overwhelmed with shame, and I never did that again.

In 1989, my husband gave me a newspaper advertisement about training to be an electrologist. Although I now realize that he knew about my problem and was offering me something that could help, at the time he presented it as a career opportunity. I was skeptical, but I still called to get more information. The trainer encouraged me and said I would get free treatment during training, so I decided I had nothing to lose.

On the first day of class, the instructor gave everyone a sample treatment so we would know how it felt. This was done in front of everyone else in the class. When my turn came, I wanted to run, to get out of there. Instead, I got on the table, sweating and nervous. It soon became apparent that the teacher couldn't get the hair out; she was trying different things, playing with the dials on the machine, and I could see she was sweating too. Then she said, "I've never seen such stubborn hair." This is someone who had done this for a living for forty years. I was devastated. To this day, I don't understand why she hadn't been more tactful and controlled the situation so my feelings could have been protected.

I don't know why or how I was able to go back the next day, but I did. Over the next five months, I spent more time being treated than I did performing the treatments on others. Some days I would spend the whole day being treated, but this experience was still valuable. I was learning how the client felt, what hurt most, and how to deal with it. I was still afraid to hope that it would work and solve my hair problem, but as graduation approached, I finally began seeing some results. I got to like the pain because I thought that if it was killing me, it had to be killing the hair as well. Luckily, today clients have the option to use topical or local anesthetic for comfort.

After my training finished later that year, I started my first clinic. Things were slow at first, which meant I didn't have the money or the opportunity to pursue my own treatments. I did have the equipment, though, so I started working on myself. I would set up two mirrors so I could see the sides of my face, and I would very slowly and patiently work on removing my facial hair. As my clinic got busier and I had less time but more money, I hired one of my classmates to come in for a full day each week to work on me. When she got pregnant, I asked my sister to train in electrolysis and shadow me; upon graduating, she worked for me and was the one to finish the work on my facial hair. By that time, I had moved on to treating my body hair as well. Some of my underarm and bikini line was done in school, but some of my bikini line I treated myself, curled over like a pretzel until my back hurt so much that I could barely straighten it.

As a perfectionist, I wasn't satisfied to just rely on my training – instead, I spent every moment experimenting and perfecting my technique. My family were my test subjects, to the point that my husband – who was always my biggest supporter – would hesitate when I'd ask him if he wanted a treatment because he knew that meant I wanted to try something out. For example, I had a theory that grey hair was only grey because it grew below the pigment layer. This theory came from a client whose grey hair grew in black after a treatment; he wasn't happy, but I was intrigued. I thought that if I undertreated grey hairs in order to stunt their growth rather than stopping it entirely, they would come back as pigmented hair. To test this theory, I asked my mom if she would let me experiment on her eyebrows, which were grey and wiry, and she agreed. Some of the hair died off that I would have preferred to come back, but all in all it was a success. I now do this as a common practice, and it works like a charm.

After being in private practice for six years, I started a government-approved vocational school, the Alberta Technical Institute of Electrolysis. I wanted to send out students into the world with more expertise than I had gained in my training, and this school helped me achieve that goal.

The next stage of my career, and of my dream to help people with unwanted hair, came when I was forty-seven. It dawned on me one day, about eight hours into my workday, that I was tired. In that moment, I realized that I wasn't getting any younger, and that there was more hair out there than I could kill in a thousand lifetimes. I had to find a way to help more people; I needed to raise an army of hair killers. With that, a seed was planted, and Jade Clinics – a franchise system – was born.

Franchising is not for the meek; it has a tough learning curve. I'm so glad I didn't know what I was getting into because I probably wouldn't have gone through with it if I had. But now, when I think of the practitioners who work in my clinics, I'm so thrilled. My heart glows as I think of how kind and caring they are, how they focus on doing the best job possible, and how they help others to feel great in their own skin. I am truly blessed to be surrounded by these amazing, wonderful souls.

The final stage of my dream is to have a clinic that is accessible to everyone suffering from unwanted hair – somewhere they can trust. All too often, people put their time, money, pain, and hope into inferior methods that leave them sad, frustrated, and still living with the hair. My fight is just beginning, though, and I know I need more warriors.

If you have an unwanted hair problem, know that you're not alone, that it's not your fault, and that there is a solution.

Before you go looking for an electrologist, there are a few things you should know. Electrolysis must be performed correctly in order to be successful, and results should be obvious within three months of regular treatment. The parameters of effective treatment are:

1. The needle is not felt when it enters the skin. The hair grows out of a hole in your skin called a follicle, and that is what the needle should be entering.
2. The current should be uncomfortable but not intolerable.
3. The hair isn't felt when being removed.
4. The practitioner should be using a microscope to ensure they are achieving these goals.

The above list helps you ensure the electrologist is accurate, which is essential to success. However, there are some safety considerations that you should look out for as well:

1. The forceps (tweezers) should be sterilized, and sterilizers should be verified to be in good order by third-party laboratories and confirmed with a spore test. Ask for the results.
2. Anything entering the skin should be disposable.
3. The treatment room should be cleaned and sanitized between clients.
4. The practitioner should use gloves.

No matter what you hear, electrolysis is the only method of permanent hair removal. Electrolysis and laser hair removal are often confused as the same technique; this couldn't be further from the truth. Electrolysis has been used for hair removal since

1869 while laser has only been around for the last twenty-five years. We know that the only side effect of electrolysis is hair loss, but its too early to know for sure if there are any adverse effects from laser. Electrolysis can and will permanently remove any hair from anywhere on anyone, while laser is not permanent and many people are not candidates. In some cases, laser can accelerate the hair growth, causing it to become bigger, deeper, and more pronounced. The laser company puts this side effect in medical terms in their fine print so that most people don't notice it. The good thing about laser hair removal is that it has made hair removal more widely accepted. People are talking about it openly and honestly without embarrassment and are wanting to get larger areas like their legs treated. And when laser doesn't give them the result they want, electrolysis does.

Nine out of ten women have unwanted facial hair, but many of them think, like I did, that they're the only one. When a client comes to me for a consultation and I can tell they feel embarrassed and uncomfortable, I want to hug them and tell them I'm going to fix this problem. Instead, I just touch their arm and say, "I understand. I was just like you once, but now I'm free." It's women like them that make me get up in the morning and attack the day, knowing I'm going to make a difference in someone's life.

It was this exact feeling that convinced my fifteen-year-old daughter, Janine, to become an electrologist. She was working for me as a receptionist one summer, and we had a client when she first started who would come into the clinic and ask to wait in a treatment room because she didn't want anyone to see her there. Then, at the end of her treatment, she would throw money on the counter and rush out the door as we'd yell after her, "Same time next week!" Within three months this same client was now sitting in the waiting area, chatting and laughing with Janine. She started dressing differently and changed her hair. She took pride in her appearance. One day, Janine came to me and said, "You don't just take out hair, you change people's lives. I want to do that too." Half an hour later, she had a needle in her hand and was starting her electrolysis career.

We don't just help women with facial hair, though. We help men with back hair who are embarrassed to take off their shirt. We help transgender individuals. And, we help people with ingrown hairs that are cystic and will need surgery if left untreated. For example, a man was once referred to me who had lost his foot in a work accident. His prosthetic had caused folliculitis so bad that he had to have his lower leg amputated, and he was now developing folliculitis in his thigh as well. We removed the hairs, and his folliculitis went away. We saved his leg.

Permanently removing unwanted hair is my passion, and I've spent the last thirty years helping others achieve this goal. It's my liberation from the eight years I spent being tormented before I finally found a solution that worked. What started as my curse has become my blessing: my unwanted hair brought me to a career in which I can truly change people's lives. If you are in a similar situation – if you have a problem in your life that seems insurmountable at times – then take steps to turn your curse into your own blessing. Take your power back and find a solution that works for you, and then share this solution with others. By doing this, you can change the world for the better.

About Jennifer Desloges

Jennifer Desloges wants to live in a world where we all feel good in our own skin. She has been a professional electrologist since 1989, has been teaching electrolysis since 1996, and is the founder and CEO of Jade Clinics. As an expert in her field, she has educated the public about unwanted hair through television, print media, speaking engagements, social media, blogs, and podcasts.

Last year, she was nominated for multiple awards for her business acumen, including "Best Small Business in British Columbia" with SBBC Awards and "Top 10 Best Franchises to Open in 2019" by Insights Success Magazine. Her business has a life of its own, fueled by her passion to end the torment of unwanted hair. Recently, Jennifer has expanded her driving force into new services, like permanent fat reduction and youth rejuvenation.

When she's not working, you can find her spending time with Marcel, her husband of thirty-nine years, as well as their children Janine and Marc, their spouses Nathan and Mika, and their three grand-dogs Princess, Bauer, and Linda – and hopefully, a few grandchildren in the future.

www.hairfreeforlife.com

5

Finding the Humour in Aging

by Terry Jackson

"Embrace the changes that come with age, keep moving, try and eat a healthy meal, and wear that plaid and polka dot outfit. JUST DO IT!"
Terry Jackson

Finding the Humour in Aging

By Terry Jackson

At first glance, I may not seem like the best person to be writing a chapter for this book. I'm a seventy-year old overweight diabetic who is living with chronic back pain, muscle loss, memory farts, and bladder issues. However, I've learned to embrace my elder years with humour, along with some amount of fortitude. I've also learned to laugh instead of beating myself up for the senior mishaps, and my life is so much better for it. By embracing the changes that come with age, I've been able to keep doing the things I love and try things that may have otherwise been impossible. Perhaps, after reading my chapter, you may be inspired to take a baby step toward trying something you never imagined you would.

The Joys of Travel

My favourite activity is sitting in my recliner, watching television, and playing games on my iPad. I could sit there for hours; it's when I feel the best. Sounds dismal, right? But it doesn't have to be. The past year has been an incredible one with many new and wonderful experiences, and it all comes from my motto: just do it!

In the back of my mind, I have always had this overriding passion to travel. In 2019, my husband wanted to take me on a fabulous trip of my choice. However, his mom's health was declining and we both knew he couldn't leave her alone. So, he instead convinced me to take a year to visit family and friends, many of whom live far away.

When I was raising my two daughters, my mindset was to push them to go to college and then to get out and see the world; to live their life the way they wanted to. And they did. Now, I whine about not seeing them (and my grandchildren) as often as I would like. My oldest is in Dubai while my youngest is in South Dakota, and I miss them. As I've aged, I've discovered how important family is to me, and I don't see them enough to suit me. Memories are the most important commodity to my husband and I – if nothing else, we can sit on the couch, remember, and laugh. I want to be a witness to the lives of my family, and I want them to be witness to my life.

So, in response to my husband's suggestion, I promptly made a list of the places and people I wanted to see: Dubai, California, South Dakota, Kansas, Idaho, England, France, and New Orleans. I've made all these trips (some of them multiple times), some on my own and some with my husband after his mom passed. Was it easy to travel alone? Oh, hell no! Was it worth it? Hell yeah!

I admit that I started flying by myself when I was much younger, so I was somewhat ahead of the curve. As the daughter of an Air Force colonel, I grew up in many different places. We were stationed in Florida, Virginia, Italy, Oklahoma, and then Virginia again when my father retired. My daughter is also a flight attendant, which has allowed me to fly on standby. As a result, I'm pretty well travelled, and I am not unfamiliar with all the ins and outs of the process. Whether it's by plane, train, or bus, I've got the confidence to push through and get where I need to be. Through these experiences, I've learned that if you get overwhelmed, you can get help by just standing in the middle of an airport concourse, train station, or bus terminal and looking helpless. It might take a bit of practice to master that look, but it is really effective. For example, when I flew back home from Dubai in April 2019, I had to pick up my luggage at Heathrow Airport in London, go through customs, and haul three bags and an oversized purse to another airline ticketing venue, all without a trolley cart. A nice American Airlines agent asked if I was okay, and if I needed help. The funny part was that I *didn't* want help that time – in fact, I was somewhat miffed that she even asked. What, did I look that bad? Old? Fat? Incapable? "I'm fine," I said as I shuffled over to the ticketing agent. I was tired and dishevelled from the seven-hour flight, but I still have a bit of stubbornness in me and I don't like to give up.

This, to me, is the key to aging and travel: you may have to push through some discomfort to make it happen, but the end result is always worth it. Also, don't be afraid to use the tools available to you. One change I've made is that I've started paying the five dollars for a little push trolley instead of being cheap and struggling with my overstuffed fifty-pound bags by myself. I have not mastered the concept of packing lighter and not taking so much stuff – I like my stuff (whether I use it or not), and clothes take up a lot more space when you're overweight. So, I use the cart. Airports also have wheelchairs and attendants who will help you to your gate and on the plane, as well as mobile people carts to drive you to your gate.

Facing these challenges can be daunting at times, but it doesn't change my enthusiasm for travel. In fact, even though I'm older, I find moving through these obstacles much smoother now. Experience often makes things easier! Sometimes, though, you have to improvise. I went to Germany with a group of friends, and one woman needed an airplane wheelchair to get down the aisle as part of her foot had been amputated due to diabetes. However, getting the chair was a slow process. During our connection in London, it was taking so long that she became worried about missing the flight to Germany – so, she crawled on her hands and knees to the cabin door. Now that's moxie!

Memory Farts

You know how it goes: you're in the middle of a sentence and can't think of a word. You don't want to just skip it and go on, so you might try to define the word in the hopes someone will help you out. It's an integral part of your ... sentence? No, idea. No ... I can't remember. I'll let you, dear reader, fill in the blank. It's an aging thing. You can't help it. It happens, and now you're afraid of getting dementia or Alzheimer's, but that's not what I'm talking about. The normal aging process simply affects your memory. To combat this, I try to keep my mind busy and challenged. I'm trying to read more and stop being on my electronic devices so much, although I've pretty much failed at putting aside my phone and iPad so far. I have

Facebook, Twitter, and Instagram accounts, and I love using them to keep in touch with my family and friends and to see pictures of my grandchildren.

While I've set a goal to be on my devices less, I do find that learning new technologies helps me challenge my mind. If I don't know how to work some new application, I ask someone younger than me for help – the younger the better! It's amazing how kids are so proficient at these "apps"; I just strive for average.

Then, there is the issue of name recall, in that I don't have any. My husband remembers faces and names, probably because he is nine and three-fourths years younger than I am. Well, that's not really true, because I never was good at remembering names and faces. I don't know why. No mnemonics scheme could save me. But you know what's great about being an elder? You can call everyone "honey" or "dear" when you can't remember a name and no one will bat an eyelash. It's a great way out of potentially embarrassing situations.

Food and Weight Loss

I've struggled with the ups and downs of weight gain and loss all my life, and I've used every possible excuse I could find. I've blamed my weight on a slow metabolism, a bad thyroid, my DNA ... all fantasy. The reality is that I don't take care of myself by eating better and exercising more. But, I am working on it. My goal is to live until I'm ninety-five, and I know I'll have a better chance of achieving that if I do something about my weight. I have to push myself to walk as I have back and sciatica pain that can be quite significant at times, but I try not to complain or make a big deal out of it. Instead, I'll find a place to sit when it flares up, and after ten minutes the pain has usually subsided and I can push on. I'm lucky that my pain will dissipate if I sit down – especially in my recliner! I am no longer able to go non-stop, though, and that's normal. Acknowledging that fact and finding ways to deal with it has kept me far more mobile than if I tried to pretend it wasn't happening or used it as an excuse to do nothing at all.

Sometimes I'm tempted to let the excuses win, but I know I have to help myself. No one's holding a gun to me and demanding that I overeat or stay in my chair. Pursuing a healthy lifestyle is hard, but I just perpetually keep trying. Some days I'm successful and some days not so much, but overall, I'm headed in the right direction.

Bladder Issues

I know this is a touchy subject, but if this isn't happening to you right now, it's most likely going to later. It's why they make adult diapers.

After two children (and sixty pounds of weight gain while pregnant), my bladder is wrecked and I can't hold my pee in as well as I used to. This problem first started showing up when I sneezed, so I came up with a technique to handle it: when I feel a sneeze coming, I stop and cross my legs. If I didn't pee my pants, success! (We elders need to take our triumphs where we can.) My daughter used to laugh her head off when she saw me do this, but then she turned fifty and discovered that her mother was probably brilliant. Now she uses the crossed-leg method too. By the way, my email is at the end of this chapter. If anyone has a more discreet option than the stop-and-cross-your-legs method, please write and let me know! Today, though, I'm usually fine until I get to the nearest ladies' room. As soon as I see a toilet and hear running water, I'm doomed. That's why they started making bladder pads; they are a lifesaver.

Another thing that has helped with this problem is that we, as human beings, are becoming more courageous in talking about these common issues. This is a good thing, because it's great to feel you're not alone.

Style and Self-Confidence

Fashionista? Not me. Never been one, never will. I do, however, admire women who can walk out their front door in clothes that hug their body and who are not intimidated by societal norms. And yes, I realize that the larger-than-necessary flowy clothes I love to wear can make one look bigger. I circumvent that problem by simply never looking at anything but my face in a mirror. But not one of those magnifying mirrors – those just show you every single life line in minute detail. My mother was not one to look at herself in a mirror either, for many of the same reasons.

There are many women in the world who can't find the self-confidence to love the way they look as they age. I look at pictures of wrinkled-faced grandmothers with their grandchildren, and my heart is touched by the look on a baby's face as they gaze into their grandma's eyes. That baby is not counting wrinkles. As I look at these pictures, I catch myself thinking how beautiful the elder's face is. So why don't I remember that when I look at myself? Probably because there are too many skinny models and face cream advertisements on TV, in magazines, and on social media. It's time that we let go of what society tells us is beautiful and embrace how we look in this moment. And part of that comes from wearing what makes us happy, whether it is "in style" or not.

I remember seeing elders wearing what I perceived to be mismatched pieces when I was young, and my thoughts about them weren't kind. Today, though, I find myself sporting outfits that would have offended my younger sensibilities. Why? Because I can! And you know what? It feels great. I get enjoyment out of the pieces I wear, and clearly other people do too. My style is quirky and unconventional, yet women come up and compliment me on an article of clothing I'm wearing or a piece of jewelry I have on.

So, go ahead and wear mismatched earrings, too much plastic jewelry, ribbons in your hair, or a purple wig – or better yet, dye your hair purple just because you can. Be proud and loud with your own style. If you become aware of any unwanted stares, know that they too will be an elder one day, and then they'll probably do the same thing.

Make the Most of It

Many of us (women especially) are brought up to be people-pleasers, and as a result we feel bad when we say no. So, we tend to say yes instead. Yes, I'll bring cupcakes, drinks, paper products, and plastic utensils for the school Christmas party. Oh, okay, I'll pick up all the girls and take them here or there. However, once we've lived long enough to be damn tired of people taking advantage of us, we find our "no" once more. We've been there, done that, and bought the t-shirt. We've spent too much time worrying about and catering to other people's needs, and now it's time to focus on what we want out of life.

On top of learning to say no to the things we don't want to do, we also need to learn to say yes to the things that bring us joy. This can be scary at times, but as you enter those golden retirement years where you finally have the time and wherewithal to do those things you always wanted to do, you need to take advantage of every single opportunity you can. For example, I'm planning on ziplining in Dubai next month on the longest zipline in the world. Am I scared? A little. But I've always wanted to know what it feels like to fly, and this is the best way I can think of to get that feeling. So, I'm saying yes to my dreams and desires, facing my fear, and taking on this challenge, going back to my motto of "just do it!"

Another time I faced my fears and found my courage was when I went with friends to Wyoming for a week-long riding retreat several years ago. The last time I had ridden a horse, I was bucked off and my entire body was bruised. On this trip, I decided it was time to face that fear of riding. By the time I arrived at the retreat, the inside of my mouth was filled with sores from anxiety. Then, the nerves in my back lit up like Christmas trees the moment I sat in the saddle. The pain was intense. I wanted to ride, though, so I kept my mouth shut and rode. Nothing worthwhile is easy. Once I got off the horse, the pain dissipated and I was fine. I rode twice a day over the seven days, determined to get over my fear of riding, and by the end of the trip I was no longer afraid. Today, the memory of the pain has faded, and I am left with only glorious memories and good feelings about what I accomplished.

Laughter is the Best Medicine

My life has always revolved around laughter. Even as a child, I would do silly things to make people laugh because it made me feel good. So, it's probably a good thing that I'm a little ditzy and graceless because it means I have funny stories to tell. I'm way beyond the slip-is-showing problem. Now, I'm into the skirt-tucked-in-the-panties problem, which is only discovered after I have left the bathroom. I also trip on my own staircase and run into furniture and then forget that I've done so. My husband will ask where I got a bruise, and I won't be able to do anything but laugh it off and say that I bumped into something.

Aging is a process of trial and error for me. I'm more on the error side, but I keep trying. I tried the vitamin thing, including to help my memory, but I kept forgetting to take them. How ironic! But the one lesson that has never failed me is learning to laugh at the mishaps – then, you can quickly move past them and onto the next thing. No one knows what the future will bring, including me, but I do know that finding humour in my day-to-day life – even if I have to laugh at myself – makes my life better.

No one's life is perfect – money or no money, family or no family, in pain or pain-free, happy or sad. We must not point the finger at anyone and think they are so lucky; I can guarantee you that there is discord in everyone's life. The way we handle our situation and our actions determines the state of our feelings. So, embrace the changes that come with age, keep moving, try and eat that healthy meal, and wear that plaid and polka dot outfit. JUST DO IT!

About Terry Jackson

Terry Jackson is of Native American and English descent. She is a grandmother who has fostered her spirituality and creativity throughout her life. She celebrates the sacredness of the feminine and shares her stories to encourage women on their own journey through life. As a global wanderer who has travelled to Machu Picchu, Egypt, Dubai, Europe, and other places near and far, Terry is an experiential learner whose life lessons have come from a variety of experiences, including being adopted and finding her birth family. She is also a certified massage therapist, aromatherapist, and hypnotherapist. She enjoys creating jewelry, writing, beading, and making lotions and potions utilizing her knowledge of essential oils.

Terry and her husband opened the only Native-owned trading post in Tucson, Arizona in 2005. Their first inventory included many pieces from their own collection, and they now have a well-stocked trading post with something for everyone. It is an anchor in the Tucson community and enjoys solid relationships with the University of Arizona, the American Indian Law School Students Association, the Tucson Indian Center, the VA Hospital, and more.

Email: azontheroadagain@gmail.com
Facebook: Terry Davidson Jackson
Instagram: @azshawnee
Twitter: @ChiMouse49

6

My Screaming Hormones

by Helen Horwat

"An imbalance in anything NEEDS to be balanced."
Helen Horwat

My Screaming Hormones

By Helen Horwat

As I sit here and begin to write this chapter, I ponder on how to begin. My story is one that is filled with curiosity, fear, challenges, and craziness, and I hope that by sharing it, I can help people in the same situation learn they are not alone.

I think the best place to start is to give you a little background about the timing of all this. I was born in the fifties, and my parents – who were both of the Depression Era – didn't offer much information on what it meant to grow up. You just did, that's all. However, I had an older sister who somehow got information from the outside world, and what she shared with me sometimes literally shocked me. One such conversation was when I learned that at some point in my teen years, I was going to become affected by something called a "menstrual cycle" – I'd had no idea that my body was going to go through such changes, and I nervously awaited their arrival.

As that time approached, I began experiencing emotions that were very out of place. I could find no rhyme or reason for them, and this bothered me. I felt how I would imagine a pet horse to feel; all he wants to do is run in the fields and be free, but instead he is trapped in a barn. One day, my sister turned to my mother and said, "Oh boy, she's cranky, I bet she's going to start soon." My mother strongly agreed with her, responding, "I hope so, because she's so out of control." I knew they were speaking about my menstrual cycle, and I too wanted it to start. I was hoping that when it did, this seesaw of emotions would finally stop. Unfortunately, it didn't start until I was sixteen – which is somewhat late – and when it did, it came with a VENGENCE.

My mother encouraged me to go see the world outside of our small town, so I left home when I was seventeen. Since we didn't have money for college, a teacher at my school encouraged me to take the civil service test, which is used to screen candidates for government positions. After successfully completing it, I was off to Washington, DC to work for the federal government. I had a job and an apartment, and my parents were so proud.

For the next two years I was on my own, and for the most part it went well. I was doing well financially, and I liked my job and my new friends. However, my menstrual cycle was never what I thought it would be. It was extremely heavy at times and the cramps were severe, but I just dealt with it. We didn't go to the doctor very often back home, so I never considered going in for this issue.

Then, I got pregnant – as responsible as I was in most parts of my life, I guess I wasn't in this aspect. At the time, abortions were just starting to be talked about on the media, and they definitely were not legal. So, I quietly found a doctor from Yugoslavia who performed abortions not far from where I worked. I don't know why, but I never suffered from any type of anguish or guilt over this decision. This was simply something that had to be done; otherwise, my life would change forever, and I wasn't ready for that. I had also known from a very young age that I did not want children. I didn't want to disappoint my parents, although they would have been loving and accepting, so I kept it a secret – no one knew about it but my boyfriend at the time and myself. But now, those of you who are reading this chapter know as well. Perhaps because both of my parents are deceased, I can say the truth out loud: I had an abortion.

After this experience, I decided to go on the birth control pill. Unfortunately, I experienced a huge increase in my appetite after starting this medication, and I gained fifty pounds over the next few months. I was doing some modelling at the time, so this weight gain was an issue. I decided to quit the birth control pill since my boyfriend was no longer in the picture, but the weight didn't drop off the way I thought it would. As someone who had been thin my whole life, I couldn't understand what was happening.

I finally went to see a doctor to get help with losing the weight, and he prescribed me some amphetamines. I had no idea that amphetamines had side effects or could be dangerous to me in any way, and I didn't ask. I trusted that my doctor knew best, and besides, I was seeing great results. I was losing weight, I was never hungry, and I was full of energy. My neighbours in the apartment building started to complain because I would be running the sweeper at two in the morning. I was taking fifty milligrams of Didrex three times a day, and I eventually learned that having a cup of coffee mid-morning and mid-afternoon would give the pills a boost – at the time, I didn't recognize this as addictive behaviour.

The best thing about the amphetamines was that I didn't suffer from my menstrual cycle when I was on them. I'm not saying the problems weren't there; I just didn't notice them. I was happy, happy, happy. I felt safe with all of this because I was under the supervision of a doctor, although I never thought to mention the issues with my menstrual cycle to him.

After about three years, I started to notice changes in my body. Some of my teeth were loose, I needed eyeglasses for the first time, and I started having anxiety attacks. So, I went back to the doctor who had been prescribing these pills to me. Before I could say anything, he asked me if I was having any trouble sleeping or if I was experiencing nervousness and then told me he could prescribe medications for those problems. At that very moment, I realized that this man had no real concern for me – that he was a pill pusher – so I politely declined and left his office, never to return. I knew I was in trouble, though, and I needed help right away.

I was now somewhat afraid of regular doctors after becoming an addict under the supervision of one, so I set up an appointment with a homeopathic doctor as soon as I could. Homeopathy embraces a holistic approach to the treatment of the sick, and this new doctor helped me come down from the addiction. He gave me B-12 shots for energy and sublingual drops to put under my tongue for the anxiety attacks. After a while, my teeth tightened up on their own and my eyesight returned to normal. My menstrual cycle remained an issue, but I was so concerned about my addiction that once again I never brought it up, instead just dealing with it the best I could.

I left my government job in 1976, five years after leaving home. My parents, I am sure, were a little nervous about this decision. I had also stopped the amphetamines, quit smoking cigarettes, stopped drinking coffee, and begun trying to maintain my weight "au natural," so perhaps they thought I had gone a little crazy. However, the truth was that I was young and curious about life, and I was tired of working with people who only talked about how much longer they had until they could retire. I was also being sexually harassed by my boss and thought it would be easier to just leave than to try and report it.

I decided to move to New York City with my new boyfriend, and it quickly became one of my favourite places. On the encouragement of my friend Eileen, I got dressed up and went to the Ford Modelling Agency, carrying a small box filled with slides of myself. Eileen went with me because I was way too shy to do this alone, especially since I truly thought we would be thrown out as we hadn't made an appointment. Surprisingly, they let us in, and before I knew it I was walking out with a five-year contract in my hand.

For the next four years, I stayed in NYC and tried to make it as a model. However, the issues with my menstrual cycle were wearing me down, although I still didn't understand how serious they were. I was struggling with my weight, and that caused me to lose modelling jobs. Eventually, I began to believe I didn't have the body for modelling. So, when my boyfriend was offered an executive position with Pepsi Cola in Mexico City, I used his move as an excuse to escape.

The next four years provided me with a much-needed opportunity to get to know myself. I didn't have a full-time job, and there wasn't the rush of the NYC streets to remind me to hurry. I went to school, I exercised, I took my vitamins, I made friends, and I adjusted to the slower pace of life. In this city, if your car or washing machine broke down, it took two weeks to get the part in – and then it was usually the wrong part, so you had to wait even longer to get it fixed.

Now that I had more time for myself, I noticed that my health fluctuated on a monthly basis. I was happy and full of energy for two and a half weeks, and then everything would slowly deteriorate over the next week. My clothes size would change in conjunction with an increase in appetite, going from a size eight to a size ten. Then, once I started my menstrual cycle, I would go back to my usual size eight. These fluctuations were a little upsetting, but I thought I just had to work on my weight a little harder. However, as the months went by, I became increasingly concerned about my situation.

Over the next few years, my health got worse. My clothes size went from an eight to a twelve every month. My appetite got scary. I became irritable towards other people; I think depression was becoming an issue. I almost felt like I was menopausal, but I was too young for that. Even though all the signs pointed to a physical cause, the doctors I contacted in the States only wanted to prescribe antidepressants, which I refused to take due to my past addiction.

By the time I was twenty-nine, I was struggling with my concentration, my patience was non-existent, and I was having crying spells. There were days when I didn't want to leave my bedroom, let alone the apartment. However, this was only true during the second half of my menstrual cycle. Within days of getting my period, I would be happy, energetic, loving life, and back in my size eight clothes. This would last for about five days after my period ended and then the cycle would start all over again, making me more and more apprehensive as the months went on. I honestly don't know why my boyfriend put up with me; I was Dr. Jekyll and Mr. Hyde.

I remember waking up one night absolutely starving. We

had a woman who cooked for us and she bought fresh groceries daily, so all I could find to eat was a loaf of bread and a jar of mayonnaise. I sat down at the table with a butter knife and ate the whole loaf, slathering mayo on each slice. When I was finally finished, I was STILL starving – it felt as though I hadn't eaten anything at all.

I was determined not to lose this battle, but I was also very tired of dealing with these problems, month after month, year after year. There were times when I got extremely down and had some bad thoughts. However, my life changed when I saw three letters on the front of a magazine: PMS.

I was sitting in the waiting area of my dentist's office when those three letters caught my eye, displayed on the front of the May 4, 1981 issue of Newsweek. I didn't know what PMS stood for, so I decided to read the article to learn more. This is where I learned of Katrina Dalton, a doctor from England who had spotted her first case of PMS (pre-menstrual syndrome) thirty years ago. One of her patients was having asthma attacks at the end of each menstrual cycle, which then would stop as soon as menstruation began. This was not the typical PMS experience – according to the article, the most common symptoms were swelling and tenderness of the breasts, bloating, acne, lethargy, tension, anxiety, depression, and heightened irritability. It went on to say that twenty to thirty percent of women suffer from symptoms that are severe enough to warrant treatment, and as many as five percent are so seriously affected that they can't function during the week or two preceding their periods.

As I read on, I learned that many experts suspected the problem involved an imbalance in the female hormones, specifically estrogen and progesterone. Dr. Samuel S. C. Yen and Dr. Robert L. Reid of the University of California proposed that women susceptible to PMS have a defect in the hormonal "messages" put out by the pituitary gland as well as a nearby region of the brain called the hypothalamus. The so-called hypothalamic-pituitary axis is the master control centre for hormones throughout the body, and it plays an important role in our emotions. To combat this defect, Dalton and her disciples prescribed natural progesterone – she stated that synthetic hormones only make the symptoms worse. Progesterone can be given by injection in severe cases or as a vaginal or rectal suppository in milder ones. Mild cases of PMS often respond to diuretics, which promote the excretion of water and relieve the bloated feeling.

By the time I was halfway through the article, tears were running down my cheeks. *It's me,* I said to myself. *They are talking about me!* Every paragraph, every word, described my exact situation. I wanted to scream, I wanted to shout, I wanted to hop a plane to England to see this doctor in person.

In June 1981, I wrote to this doctor and poured my heart out, explaining my symptoms and how they had progressively gotten worse over the past ten years. Less than a month later, I received a letter from Dr. Dalton. She thanked me for my letter and said:

"In answer to your question, if you find natural progesterone in suppository form, it will be quite safe for you to try without a doctor's supervision. However, I would advise you to ensure that the suppositories are of NATURAL progesterone and not made of one of the synthetic progestogens. Full particulars are contained in my book *Once A Month* published by Hunter House, Pomona, California. You may be interested to know that in the States there is a 'PMS Action' group and if you contact them, they may well be able to help you further."

Amazingly, the PMS clinic she was referring me to was located just fifty minutes from where I grew up as a child. Help was right on my doorstep; I just hadn't known it was there! If this information had been more readily available back then, I would not have had to suffer the way I did.

I used progesterone for the next twenty-four years (only stopping when I had my last menstrual cycle at the age of fifty-two) and the difference in my quality of life was incredible. This truly changed and saved my life. I regained my energy, my positive outlook on life, and my size eight body, and I kept them throughout my entire cycle. My boyfriend at the time (we have since split up) felt like he had met a new woman, and he was so grateful to Dr. Dalton. This was not a temporary, artificial fix by a chemical substance with a myriad of side effects; this was a long-term solution that corrected a simple hormone imbalance.

This new balance in my physical being made me whole again and put me back in control of my life. Now that I was no longer stuck on this hormonal rollercoaster, I was able to go on to do many things. At sixty-six years old, I have owned and operated a state-licensed modelling school. I have raised my nephew, who is now thirty-eight, from the age of six. I was hired by American Airlines as a flight attendant and have travelled the world numerous times. I have bungy jumped, skydived, and raced snowboards. I own motorcycles. I run four miles a day.

When we wake up each morning (unless we have become totally helpless), we have a choice to make. Whether we are alone or with a partner, whether we are sick or healthy, we make a decision as to how the day is going to start. True quality of life is knowing how to be in control of your destination, and it all starts with your mindset. So, find whatever it takes to give each day a positive start and do it. If you have to cry or ask for help from a friend, that's okay. If you have health issues that you have to learn how to manage, then find someone you can trust and work with them. If you need to change your partner, your job, or your city, make the change. Find the balance in your own life – physically, mentally, and emotionally – and never, ever give up on yourself.

About Helen Horwat

Helen (Chome) Horwat was born in Brownsville, PA in 1953. She went on to become a recruiter for the US Information Agency in Washington, DC and then became a certified expert examiner through the state department. She also trained as a graphic artist and was privileged to work on the America Illustrated Russian Magazine, which is now a part of the John Marsh Files at the Gerald R. Ford Presidential Library.

Despite being a shy child who was terribly bullied, Helen was gifted with great bone structure and a tall, lean figure that was perfect for modeling. She became a model with the Ford Modeling Agency in NYC in 1977 and later went on to open her own state-licensed modeling school, Finesse. She also became a lecturer and motivational speaker on the topics of dressing for success, job interviewing techniques, and promoting yourself through your resume.

In her personal life, Helen raised her nephew from the age of six and was the caregiver for both of her parents in their final years. She has spent the last thirty-three years working for American Airlines as a flight attendant, enabling her to do what she enjoys most: travel the world and be there for her passengers.

Email: chomehorwat@mac.com

7

Live Young as Old as Possible!

by Marlies White

"It's not how well you've lived that really matters,
but how many lives have lived well because
you lived!"
Rajesh Murthy

Live Young as Old as Possible!

By Marlies White

I love stories, both hearing them and sharing them, and the story I want to share is about my baby, SomaLife. So many people are part of this chapter of my life, but the most brilliant spotlight is reserved for my husband who changed so many lives for the better – mine included! And so, with the utmost admiration, love, and respect, I tell this story as a tribute to my husband, Dr. Philip White.

Philip was a born healer. Born and raised in England, he told his mum at just three years old that he wanted to be a doctor and help people. Throughout the years, his talent and determination led him towards this goal. After getting his start in internal medicine (focusing on research for cell repair and regeneration, the body's natural healing factors, aging, and longevity), he decided he would achieve a wider field of treatment by switching to family medicine. He was a brilliant family doctor, as evidenced by the positive impact he had on so many people's lives. The babies he delivered eventually went on to have children of their own, whom he delivered as well. I felt such a warmth knowing that his patients loved and trusted him.

Always wanting to be on the cutting edge of medicine, Philip chose to continue his research even after the switch, working on developing ways to help the body slow down the aging process. He possessed such a vast amount of knowledge, and I really believed he could help everyone live longer with his simple, effective, natural approaches.

About now, you are probably wondering how I met such an incredible man. After immigrating to Canada at the age of six, I started Grade One without knowing a word of English. Youngsters learn quickly, though, and I was soon accepted by my peers. I grew up loving the English language, even writing small articles for my school that were printed in the local newspaper on a regular basis. My parents couldn't afford to send me to university when I finished high school, so I first trained as a hairdresser and then got a job at a major bank years later. I worked my way up from my first position as a teller to become an account manager for loans, mortgages, and investments, and it was here that I met Philip. He had been referred to me by a mutual acquaintance, and after chatting for a bit, he asked me if I would like to go flying with him sometime. Flying in a small plane sounded scary yet exciting, so of course I accepted. I quickly learned that yes, it was scary – especially for someone with a fear of heights! However, as our relationship developed, I wanted to be part of Philip's passion for flying. So, I put my fear aside and managed to get my pilot's license.

I remember my initial training flight with my instructor.

The plane vibrated as we raced down the runway, getting ready to lift off. It felt like the bottom would drop out at any minute. I was scared, but I did my best to calm myself down and push through. After about forty hours of training, I was finally sent off on my own to do one solo circuit. While this was a real accomplishment, I never really enjoyed flying enough to be able to call it a passion.

An important part of the training involved learning how to recover from stalls and spins. Although I didn't really care for either manoeuvre, the reason for practicing these skills became apparent one ice-cold Sunday morning. Philip and I wanted to go on our usual weekend flight for breakfast in Oliver, which is located just south of Kelowna. This was one of our coldest winters ever – the temperature was forty degrees below zero – and the plane had been stored in a warm hangar, so we pulled it out and did our walk-around, checking for loose bits and testing for water in the fuel line. Everything looked good, so we got in, got clearance from the tower, and flew off.

We were still climbing when a sudden hush fell over the cabin, leaving only the soft sound of the air passing by the cockpit as the propeller slowed to a lazy turn. The engine had quit! I turned to Philip, white-knuckled and scared, and I could tell that he was concerned too. I quietly grabbed onto the edge of my seat, thinking to myself, *If we are going to crash, I will not go down screaming. I will die with dignity.*

Philip had to make a split-second decision. Should he try to belly the plane onto the frozen lake about half a mile from the end of the runway, or should he turn around and glide the plane back to the airport? Deciding on the runway, he put the plane into a gentle left turn and radioed the tower to inform them of our situation.

As we neared the runway, everything seemed to unfold in

slow motion. Emergency vehicles raced alongside us, ready to assist, as we floated toward the ground. Then, just as Philip was about to set the plane down, the engine sprang to life and he had to make some quick adjustments to counter the power surge, averting another potential disaster. Moments later, we were finally safely down. We later determined that during our climb, an ice plug had formed in the fuel line. Fuel starvation had almost done us in, but with focus and determination, we were able to make a successful landing. Philip was truly my hero that day!

What brought Philip and I together was our love of adventure and our interest in helping others. Our love for adventure is what got me into flying, as well as scuba diving, golf, fishing, and skiing. However, it was our interest in helping others that would take us down an incredible path.

The first phase of what I began to think of as our adventure began in 1998 in the basement of our home. I turned fifty that year, and although Philip and I were both still very active in our professional lives, we started thinking about how we would transition into our retirement when the time came. At first we were unsure what direction to take, but then the terminal illness of a family member became the catalyst to take action. I asked Philip, "With all of your years of medical and scientific research, could you create a product to help people live healthier and longer lives?"

Knowing my passion for helping others, Philip spent a considerable amount of time doing research based on medical studies, such as the ones conducted by Dr. Terry and Dr. Chein as well as the Rudman Study to name just a few. The data showed that between the ages of twenty-five and sixty, our levels of human growth hormone (HGH) decrease significantly. After the age of sixty (or sometimes earlier), the effects begin to show. You don't feel as energetic or recover as quickly as you did in your younger years. You feel more tired than usual, and you look in the mirror and see those "laugh lines." Philip's aim was to target the body's natural ability to increase HGH levels, and so he focused on figuring out a specific combination of amino acids which could help the body do just that. And, he succeeded! Based on previous studies as well as his own research, Philip developed a powerful supplement designed to slow the aging process by assisting the body in naturally repairing itself at a cellular level. The product was patented as "Youth Formula," and with that, SomaLife was born!

Philip, with his commitments to his medical practice, did not have the luxury of time to be hands-on in SomaLife. So, it was up to me to determine the setup and operation of the business. During the first two years, I worked twelve hours a day or more, unfortunately sacrificing my social life in the process. I have since learned that you can't buy time, and I regret now that family and friends became a missing piece in my life.

Eventually, we reached the point where more staffing was needed for the company to grow. As a practicing physician, Philip was restricted from endorsing or representing the product he had created. So, how could we share this amazing formula? To answer this question, we set about trying to find qualified staff to help us.

First, I approached the people who had already tried the product – our SomaLife family – and their involvement quickly became a grassroots movement. However, as SomaLife continued to grow, we started to look for professionals to market and manage the company. Unfortunately, Philip put too much trust in the professionals who approached us to build the brand, and it seemed like everyone we hired had their own agenda for how our funds should be utilized. By this time the reins had been handed to others, and I was only asked to participate in the company's operations in order to provide funding to keep the company alive, which I did. This was still my baby – even though it now had foster parents in the guise of outside management – and I was not about to give up. I have always been steadfast in never giving up on something I believed in, even at my own expense ... literally.

We had gone through three different CEOs and were just starting to revisit our options for the future of SomaLife when Philip was diagnosed with a terminal illness. I spent the next two and a half months caring for him, but sadly my husband the healer could not heal himself. At the end of 2015, less than three months after his diagnosis, my husband of thirty years passed away and my heart shattered. I didn't know what the future held without Philip by my side.

After Philip's death, my life took a turn for the worse. I never understood why, but shortly before he passed Philip had handed the company over to a marketing guru who promised to manage the company and elevate its brand worldwide, without Philip receiving compensation of any kind. The company was now down from a staff of seventeen to a staff of three: the marketer, me, and one customer service representative. I had no idea what my role in the company was – my claim to fame was seemingly just being Dr. White's wife, as well as the person who provided money to the company when needed.

I had never been comfortable with any of the management we hired as I felt they put me on a back burner, and this marketer was no exception. He was very charming, but I felt he was secretly glad that Philip did not have oversight on him anymore. Everything was always about money! After Philip's death, the marketer started to ask me for personal loans, which made me feel uncomfortable. I thought I was helping him at first, but eventually I felt he was using me as his personal ATM. He would always flash up a note with repayment terms, but those payments never came. Asking me for a "loan" to pay off his mortgage in the US was the last straw. He always said he wanted to keep his family out of harm's way, but what about me?

This is when I finally started asking questions. Why was he asking me for a personal loan to pay off his mortgage in the US? Also, why couldn't he travel to the States, and why did he not have any ID showing he was a Canadian resident? I had known that he travelled on an Irish passport, yet he was reluctant to provide me with any further identification, which had never been requested before. It was time to go see a lawyer. I finally found my voice and confronted the marketer, after which he simply didn't return to work. Thankfully, the marketer's departure ended up being a positive change for the company as I could now do SomaLife 2.0 on my terms. I soon realized I'd had the ability to control and manage the company all along; I didn't need to put my trust in outside interests.

I was now able to move into the next phase of this story, which involved taking control of the company again. So many years of pain and not seeing my baby flourish were coming to an end!

You might be wondering what drove me to support the company through all that happened – why I didn't just give up and let it die. One reason is that I never give up, but another is that I was the original guinea pig for our youth product. I started taking it when I began to feel the effects of aging in my late forties, and I was excited to find that I was immediately sleeping better, my hair and nails improved, and I had so much more energy. I haven't stopped aging, but I'm doing it slowly and with more energy than I ever expected.

Because of the formula that Philip developed, I have been able to enjoy things that may not have been otherwise possible. Philip and I had joined a dragon boat team together in 2000, and I eventually went on to win a gold medal with the senior's team at the BC Senior's Games in 2008, along with numerous other medals. I also steered on several women's teams, frequently "bringing home the gold." In 2016, I finally retired as the oldest female steerer on the lake to make room for other passions.

This energy also extended to being able to do more community work. I was always looking for ways to make a difference, so when I came upon an ad put out by the RCMP looking for people to assist the regular officers in community policing, I applied and became one of the first three female auxiliary constables in BC. The training was rigorous, with self-defence and firearms training, and at the end I was able to assist with performing roadside and traffic checks, policing the downtown area, and performing some administration work for the officers I worked with. I enjoyed this time immensely.

Having more energy has also allowed me to explore several hobbies that may not be typical for a woman my age. When I was well into my fifties, I purchased a bright yellow Viper. One year I was asked to do the parade lap at the Molson Indy, and I drove Kane, the American wrestler, around the track just prior to the actual race. I would also race other like-minded Viper owners on the Vernon racetrack. Seeing smoke billow from the screaming tires was exhilarating!

In 2017, my sixty-ninth birthday was a non-event as friends and family had made other plans. So, I decided to buy a Harley Davidson. Philip and I had both owned scooters, but I had sold them after he passed away. Now that I was staring down my seventies, I felt the need to get back on the road. I had the

Harley delivered to my home as I didn't have a clue how to ride it – the scooters had been automatic, as had the Honda 650 I had once owned, so I needed to learn how to change gears. I was introduced to a motorcycle instructor who felt that I would only need a couple of hours of instruction since I already had a motorcycle license, and he was right. For the past two years, I have ridden my Harley whenever possible. There is a large biker community in Kelowna, and groups of us go for rides all over this beautiful province of British Columbia. I am living life, enjoying new friends, and continuing to turn back the clock ... sometimes at a great rate of speed.

So much has changed over the course of my story. When Philip and I first started SomaLife in 1998, I was not experienced enough to take on the enormous challenge of running a company. Yet somehow, SomaLife and I both survived. This company has always been my baby, and everything I went through to get here has made me better.

At the end of the day, it all boils down to three things: what is more important, what is less important, and what is not important at all. SomaLife was important to me, and it started with a vision to make a difference in the lives of others. Making the vision a reality the past twenty-two years has taught me the following:

1. Beware of wolves in sheep's clothing! Trust everyone, but verify that what they say is true.
2. Never give up. Be fierce in your commitment to succeed.
3. Even if it takes time, prepare yourself to step into YOUR power. You are enough, and you can do this!

While SomaLife has always been my baby, none of this would have been possible without Philip. His "Youth Formula" has been Kelowna's best kept secret for so many years, and I have made it my mission to share my vision and Philip's legacy with the world.

Philip, I've got this!

"Never dismiss old people having fun; you will be one of them eventually if you're lucky."
Carmine Savastano

About Marlies White

Marlies White was inspired to start her business, SomaLife, in response to the loss of a close relative. Working with her husband, Dr. Philip White MD, the pair created a series of products directed at promoting better health for others. SomaLife is an Okanagan-based health, wellness, nutrition, and age management company that develops, manufactures, and markets its proprietary line of one-of-a-kind products locally, nationally, and internationally. Now with over two decades of experience under her belt, Marlies leads her company to grow with the vision of changing more lives with natural health and wellness products.

Marlies is active in her community, especially with the local food bank and the Kelowna SPCA. The company's SomaPet supplement was specifically created because of her love of animals. Marlies lives by her personal motto of "You do what needs to be done, whatever it takes, helping as many people as possible along the journey." Knowing how important her company is, she looks forward to fulfilling her husband's legacy in the coming years.

www.somalife.com

8

Disconnected Motherhood CAN be Reversed

by Michelle Berezan

"Being a mother is learning about strengths you didn't know you had and dealing with fears you never knew existed."
Linda Wooten

Disconnected Motherhood CAN be Reversed

By Michelle Berezan

It's Christmas Eve 2012, and I am pregnant. After enduring multiple early miscarriages, I've finally made it to the last few days of the first trimester. I can't believe all my dreams are about to come true – that I'm finally going to become a mother.

Then, at 2:00 a.m., I'm awoken by a horrible, debilitating pain. I need to get to the bathroom, but I can't stand. Holy shit, this pain won't stop. I'm losing him. I manage to get to the bathroom and the bleeding is starting. I suddenly become lifeless as I watch my baby and insides bleed out of me. I'm powerless over what is happening within my body, and the emotional pain is not enough to overpower the physical pain. At some point, I make it back to bed and pass out from the physical pain of what's just transpired.

At 7:00 a.m. on Christmas morning, I walk into my parents' kitchen for what is about to be the worst day of my life. My dad takes one look at me and asks what happened. As tears run down my face, I manage to utter the words, "I lost the baby." I can't feel my dad's arms around me because my body is numb.

I spend the next two days in and out of the hospital, ensuring that my body has successfully terminated my baby. The painful reality of that statement rings in my ears as I turn into a hollow shell of a woman. The "why" question doesn't even cross my mind, because I know the answer. Due to recurring endometriosis and cervical cancer, my reproductive organs had been left with a lot of scar tissue, rendering my eggs defective (as the reproductive specialist put it). My dreams of becoming a mother seemed to be eluding me.

After my body recovered from the trauma of losing yet another baby, I wanted a definitive answer as to whether or not my dream of biological motherhood was still attainable. I decided to visit a specialist, who had me undergo testing to find out if I was capable of becoming pregnant and carrying a healthy baby to term. This process was emotional, frustrating, and painful. Every test came back with a worse result than the last, and one test in particular was excruciating. This is the part that always magnifies my frustration: a male doctor performing a physically painful test on a woman's most sensitive area and discounting her pain. I mean, the instruments he used … when I first walked into the operating room, I thought it was a display set up to show people the torturous instruments they used on women throughout history. When they told me that it was all set up for me, I almost ran from the room. I did take a step back from the table in hesitation, but the desire to have a baby overtook my instincts to run.

My journey to become a single mother by choice included

extensive testing, poking, prodding, hormone injections, thousands of dollars, and hours upon hours of contemplation. You see, coming to this decision to proceed into motherhood on my own meant I had to give up on the ideation of "family" I had in my head, which was extremely difficult for me. Looking back now, I can see that I made the best decision I could with the information I had – no one could have predicted the emotional and mental torture I would suffer over the next six years.

With all of this time, money, and effort, you would think that I would have been ecstatic when I finally delivered a healthy baby. I thought I would be overcome with this amazing love, but when I looked down at my beautiful, sweet baby boy, I felt nothing. At that moment, I felt like I had potentially made the biggest mistake of my life.

Over the next few weeks, tears flooded my eyes on a daily basis. I cried over the lack of joy and the fear that I shouldn't have gone to so much trouble to become a mother. I was inundated with the "why" questions. Why did I force this to happen? Why did I want to be a mother so badly? Why didn't anyone tell me it would be like this? Why did everyone make such a big deal about motherhood? Why do all the movies make having a baby seem like the most wonderful experience a woman could ever have? I had an easy baby. I had a sweet baby. I had a beautiful baby. I wished I hadn't had a baby. And that statement, that last one right there, would continue to haunt me for days ... weeks, months, years.

Time for some scientific education. The "baby blues" is a term most people are familiar with – it is used to describe the sadness a woman may experience due to a severe hormonal change after giving birth to a child, which usually does not linger beyond a few weeks. Perinatal depression, previously referred to as prenatal/postpartum depression, is a similar condition that covers a more severe set of symptoms lasting over a much longer time frame. According to BC Women's Hospital, the term "perinatal depression" describes a woman who experiences feelings of extreme sadness, anger, irritability, guilt, worthlessness, hopelessness, and being completely overwhelmed during her pregnancy or after giving birth to her baby.

For myself, I experienced perinatal depression after the loss of my Christmas baby, which then continued throughout my pregnancy and increased after giving birth to my first child. My saving grace was a public health nurse in Salmon Arm, BC, who happened to give me a workbook on postpartum depression. I didn't think that I actually had depression – I just thought I was still grieving – but I quickly followed the suggestion of cutting caffeine, gluten, and sugar from my diet. Apparently, caffeine and sugar stimulate the central nervous system, which then causes feelings of depression. Within a month or two, I felt like a new woman, and I started actually loving my child.

Now that I was beginning to enjoy motherhood, I decided that I wanted my son to have a sibling. And truthfully, I also wanted to experience having a baby without that horrific depression. Okay, maybe that wasn't the brightest reasoning, but I was still a little insane at the time and completely unaware of it.

Unfortunately, when I was pregnant with my second child, I experienced depression so intense that I went so far as to plan my own suicide! Upon sharing this information with my parents during a very heated discussion about my behaviour, my dad immediately took me to the emergency room at the hospital. I spent three hours being assessed by a psychiatrist, who informed me that I was experiencing perinatal depression caused by an imbalance of my hormones, and that I had been suffering from this off and on since the loss of my Christmas baby. Many ask the question, "How did you not realise what was happening to you?" This is where lack of education on mental illness comes into play. Most people who are experiencing symptoms of severe depression or manic behaviour are often unaware of how bad it is while it is happening. I am a bright, vibrant woman who has never experienced clinical depression. I also thought postpartum depression only occurred after you deliver a baby, so I didn't think it applied to what I was feeling during pregnancy. This is why changing the term from prenatal/postpartum depression to perinatal depression is so much better – having an all-encompassing term can help women avoid missing a potentially early diagnosis.

This particular psychiatrist's solution was to put me on medication. When I asked how it would affect the baby currently growing in my tummy, he told me it was the "least harmful drug I could take." I questioned the words "least harmful," then proceeded to search the internet for possible side effects. It's odd how I went from planning my suicide to wanting to protect my baby at all costs. This is why perinatal depression is so obscure – it comes and goes with the ever-changing hormones that happen throughout pregnancy and after delivery. This is also why it is so tough to treat organically.

During my research, I read that the most common side effects were all of the symptoms I was currently experiencing. When I brought up my concerns that the drug would most likely magnify my current suicidal thoughts and harm my so-far healthy baby, the doctor dismissed them. I left the hospital feeling more alone and isolated than ever before, but I still did not fill the prescription. Not once was that workbook brought out, even when I went to an appointment with the "top specialist in the field." I put that in quotations because she was fresh out of school and in no way qualified to be the top of her field – as it turned out, she was just the head of the new department. Not one of these specialists were able to provide me with any solutions. Feeling this isolated was not exactly conducive to raising a toddler while pregnant; I am actually surprised that even my parents left me alone with him. It is so important for women to have support, especially when experiencing perinatal depression – or any kind of depression for that matter.

At seven months pregnant, I decided to pursue my practicum options out of town so that I could finish my master's degree in psychology prior to giving birth to my second child. Oh, did I forget to mention that I decided to go back to school a month before I gave birth to my first child? This turned out to be a good thing, though, because I learned how to help myself as well as others. I was able to finish my practicum two days before I gave birth. I then went back on the special diet to help myself deal with the depression, and I exercised like crazy! Thankfully the depression wasn't as bad this time around, which led me to believe I was done with all that negative emotion.

I was almost back to my regular weight and emotional state when I received a bill for storing the three remaining embryos left after my second baby. Rather than continue paying for storage, I decided to leave it up to fate and see what happened. One embryo did not survive the thawing process, so they implanted the remaining two inside of me. One didn't take, but the other one split into two! I was now going from two children to four in a very short time frame. The pressure of the two babies on my lower extremities became excessive early in the pregnancy, which resulted in me having to give up my extreme exercise regime. This quickly prompted the depression to start setting back in.

Nothing could have prepared me for giving birth to two premature babies, who arrived four days after my first child turned four. I had to have a caesarean birth because Baby B wasn't cooperating with her positioning, and this was an entirely different experience than the natural births I experienced with my first two children. It was awful. From the moment the needle went into my back to freeze my body from the chest down, that "extreme sadness" began to set in. Unfortunately, it didn't get any better when I brought my identical twin girls home. I had two days a week of daycare for my two boys, but I was on my own the rest of the time. Sure, I had a few relatives who gave my boys rides to daycare and swimming lessons, but that wasn't all I needed.

The lack of help after giving birth was in part due to my anger and irritability, which was directed at anyone within earshot. Looking back now, I am honestly surprised that all my children and I survived that first year and a half. No one knew the symptoms of perinatal depression, and so no one understood how harmful it was to leave me alone. Without anyone else there for me to direct my anger at, my boys became the poor souls who had to endure those intense outbursts. This is where my deepest shame comes from. I yelled at my little boys. I spanked my little boys. I scared my sweet little boys. I damage my little boys' spirits. I became my worst nightmare. I will forever remember the painful memories I instilled in my two beautiful boys, as well as in my girls who witnessed every terrible act.

Thankfully, as I write this, I can tell you I have stopped yelling at my kids. I have stopped spanking my kids. I love my kids more than anything in the world, and I would do anything to protect them. I actually love being a mommy now. How did I get from secretly wanting to harm myself out of fear of harming my children to this place of deep, profound love?

The lesson I needed came when I was seven months pregnant with my twins. I had just been abruptly cut off by three of my closest friends, who were a good chunk of my support system. I felt like I was completely alone on my journey. I was driving down the road, bawling my eyes out, when I received a phone call from a trusted and very spiritual friend. She told me that I would not receive the help I wanted from the physical realm, but I would definitely receive everything I needed and wanted from the spiritual realm. This may sound hokey to some of you, but to me, it was divine intervention. That call came to me at the exact moment I needed it. I had been exercising my spiritual connection off and on throughout my entire life, so my friend's suggestion was a solution I could grab onto quite easily.

Ever since that call, I have embraced my connection with my Higher Power and my ancestors, and it has been my saving grace in more instances than I can count. For example, I remember trying to put all the kids to bed one night about two weeks after my girls were born. The girls were both screaming and the boys were acting out – my volatile parenting at the time was creating even more misbehaviour. Overwhelmed, I sat down on the stairs in tears and begged my deceased grandmothers to please help me. Within seconds I felt my grandmothers in the room, and moments after that the babies both magically stopped crying. Whether anyone believes me or not is irrelevant because I know my truth, and I stand in it.

With the help of spiritual advisors, I have repaired my relationship with my boys. I plan lots of activities with my kids, we all snuggle daily, and we love doing arts and crafts together on the weekends. However, as a working single mother, I quickly discovered that my children needed to start helping me around the house at an early age. So, my children help me clean the house, vacuum, fold and put away laundry, load and empty the dishwasher, prepare meals and snacks, and so on. When my stress levels are high, I ask them to play quietly so I can have some quiet time to calm down. I have taught my boys to "criss-cross apple sauce and three deep breaths" – which means to sit on a cushion, cross your legs, and take three deep breaths when you get angry – and I do the same thing alongside them.

Part of my anger and irritability stemmed from others' comments and/or judgements. I have since come to terms with my life choices and am extremely grateful for all of my children and everything we have accomplished as a family. I have realised that I am a miracle – I defied all odds and gave birth to four healthy children between the ages of thirty-eight and forty-two. I no longer care what others think about my parenting. I am not a perfect parent, nor am I the worst; I am simply doing the best I am capable of, just like my children. And in the end, a perfect parent is not some description of everything you "should" be doing – a "perfect parent" is a parent who loves their children unconditionally and shows them this on a daily basis.

Presently, I feel more alive and settled with who I am than ever before. In changing my views of motherhood and how I want to live my life, I have begun attracting more positive, like-minded people. The friends I have now will definitely last a lifetime. I have also developed a strong reputation in my private practice of life coaching, addictions counselling, and perinatal counselling. And, I am now a parenting coach. Wow! I went from being what I thought was the worst mother in the world to a coach for other parents who are struggling.

There were a few changes I made in my life that allowed this transformation to happen. Through practicing healthy eating habits – including lowering my caffeine and sugar intake – and a consistent vigorous exercise regime, I have been able to feel good on the inside and the outside. A healthy body is a healthy mind, or so the saying goes.

In addition, by developing my relationship with my Higher Power, I have been able to alter my negative mindset into a more positive thinking model. Positive actions can help alter any disconnected mother into a more thriving mother. My Higher Power allows me to be me – energetic, flawed, funny, out-of-the-box, and vibrant! I love myself through the eyes of my Higher Power, and I am deeply grateful for this connection and resounding belief.

I am grateful that I will be able to teach these life strategies to my children from an early age, which will enable them to build lifelong friendships with each other and those who will cross paths with them in the future. This is an amazing gift to give to my children, and it is reassuring to know that they will never feel as alone as I did, even after I leave this world. They will always have their relationship with their Higher Power, however they define that in the future, and with each other. This I will do right as a mother.

I also want to address the women who are unable to have biological children of their own. It doesn't matter how you become a mother, your children will still inherit most of their behaviours from you – shit! And to the women who choose not to become mothers, I applaud you. It takes deep soul searching, and it takes a powerful woman to live her own truth.

About Michelle Berezan

Michelle Berezan is a therapeutic life coach, counsellor, speaker, author, and supermom of four children – including twins! Combining her formal education and extensive life experience, she specializes in successfully treating addictions, issues with self image, perinatal depression, parental obstacles, and stress. Through her private practice, Michelle helps individuals discover and expand upon the positive aspects of their lives, thus enriching their lives further. She also uses her experience as a mother of high-spirited children and multiples to pass on firsthand knowledge of how to overcome stressful parenting situations and build a strong family unit. It is her passion to speak to young people and to inspire women of any age to find their joy and passion in life.

Michelle has spoken at residential dependency treatment centres about her own journey of overcoming addiction as well as on improving one's own life condition through personal accountability and giving back. She has hosted many successful charity events and has travelled to Ghana and Egypt on charitable endeavours. Michelle makes it a priority to be of service both locally and abroad through her foundation SWAG (Service Work Around the Globe), and she continues to speak out about improving your life not only after addiction but also after perinatal depression in her latest book, which should be finished shortly.

www.MichelleBerezan.com

9

The Best is Yet to Come

by Kristy Henkes-Joe

"Live life, take chances, and don't wait, because right now is the oldest you've ever been and the youngest you will ever be again!"
Suzanne Collins

The Best is Yet to Come

By Kristy Henkes-Joe

Have you ever dreaded turning a certain age? I have. Growing up, it was so much fun to become a teenager at thirteen, to celebrate my sweet sixteen, and to reach the legal age of nineteen. Then, as people began to turn twenty, then twenty-five, then thirty, they began to joke that they were SO old! But to me, turning forty always seemed to be a big deal. Everyone who turned this age was told they were "over the hill," and they would be given canes, denture cream, and adult diapers at their parties. As a result, I dreaded turning forty when I was young because I saw it as being the time when you became an old person. However, as I got closer and closer to that milestone, I came to a realization: why couldn't we be more like children, counting down the days until our birthday because we just can't wait to celebrate ourselves? It's your birth date – the day a very powerful ceremony occurred where your mother brought you from the spirit world to the physical world. It's the day a legend was born!

I have always been an innovator – a mover and shaker who thinks outside the box. So, when I turned forty this year, I took a different approach. Standing at the top of the "hill," I had the best view to pause and look down to see that this hill was actually a huge mountain. The literal last chapter of my life – which I wrote about in the previous book in the Woman Of Worth series – involved dealing with my post-traumatic stress disorder that came from compound trauma. My mental, physical, emotional, and spiritual beings were all unhealthy, and over the past ten years I have been defragmenting my brain and finding my true, authentic self. From this new vantage point, I could see how far I have come and be proud of that climb. I could also turn and look down the other side to see all the things I want to do and all the potential adventures that lay before me. It's time to enjoy life and have fun going back down that mountain!

I feel more confident now than I did in my younger years because I have learned A LOT of life lessons over the past forty years. I've learned to stop thinking about what everyone else wants or thinks and to put up healthy boundaries. I've learned to take my power back by rejecting all the brainwashing about what is right, what is wrong, who is worthy, who is not, what religion to follow, and more. And, I cemented my belief that no person is worth more than another. We are all human beings with a soul, and we are all one. We all deserve to love, to be loved, and to be accepted into society as equals. Unfortunately, for many people – myself included – this lesson is learned the hard way.

Have you ever sat there and wondered, how did I get to

this place? And how can I ever get out of this mess alive? You started on a path, and even though you saw a few red flags, you kept going. Then the stakes got bigger and bigger, and you were pulled into a vortex of hurt, sadness, anger, and jealousy. You feel unhappy, lost, hurt, and regretful, and the effects start to show up in your work, your home life, your relationships, and your decisions. This was the story of my first marriage. I got married at the age of twenty-four and had two children by the age of twenty-eight, in part because that is what everyone is "supposed" to do. Society dictates that you should graduate high school, go on to finish college, get married, and have kids, in that order. I know now that we all have different purposes and journeys in life, but at the time I was still brainwashed by the messages from my upbringing.

I now say my first marriage was a lesson on what didn't work and the beginning of my questioning of our society's belief system around how our lives should be lived. I remember always being alone during my marriage, and while I might not have been alone physically, that's the way I felt emotionally. Then, one day I woke up alone again with the babies to take care of and knew my marriage was over. I couldn't keep living in this toxic situation. My husband and I had grown far apart in regard to our values and priorities in life; we wanted different things and had different goals. I had been doing everything I could to make this relationship work, but I had reached the end of my rope, and I could see that holding on was more painful than letting go. So, I took the first steps toward separating from my husband.

When he got home that day, he seemed to immediately understand what was happening, and he didn't even fight my decision. Sometimes the right answer is so obvious, but you block it from your mind so you don't have to deal with the feelings and consequences that would come with it.

At first, I pushed down the sadness that came with the end of my marriage. I felt like such a failure, and like I was a bad mother because I couldn't keep the family together. These feelings of regret, anger, hate, sadness, and jealousy came from my inner messages of "you are not good enough," "you are insignificant," "you are not worthy," "you are not beautiful," and "you are not smart" – all beliefs that stemmed from the society I grew up in. I didn't have time to be sad, though; I had my beautiful children to take care of. However, as I reflected on my situation, I brought awareness to myself and realized how unhappy I had been in my marriage. I was stuck in survival mode, making sure the bills were paid, the diapers and milk were bought, and the kids were fed and bathed. All the days seemed to be the same, and I had gotten so caught up in other people's worlds that I had lost myself. Something had to change. At the time, my motivation for embarking on my healing journey was to be a better mother for my children. I have since realized that I should have done it for myself first and foremost, but I was in such an unhealthy state at the time that I could not love myself. Sometimes we have to accept the motivations that got us started on our healing journeys and to realize we did the best we could with what we knew at the time. We have to love ourselves and others for where we are in life.

To get started on my healing journey, I had to take accountability for my decisions, actions, and consequences. So, I went on a mission to find my purpose and intention, to let go of the hurt, and to reverse those negative inner voices. At this point, I remembered that a family member had gone to a personal and professional development seminar called Choices, and it sounded like exactly what I needed right now. I called her up to get more information, and after some saving and fundraising, I was off.

The seminar was the kickstart I needed to get out of my zombie-like, lifeless state. Over the course of five days, I was given life tools that I could use to get through tough times, and I was shown how to let go of the "baggage" I had been carrying that made my life heavy. It was amazing to see how light and free I felt once I was able to let go. I also did exercises and went through processes to find my purpose in life, and I finally discovered it: I am a strong, beautiful, confident woman who leads others to reach their full potential so they will find peace, love, and happiness from within. And now that I know my purpose, I work with it every day. On the hard days – when my negative inner voices start screaming at me, creating feelings of anger and sadness – I remind myself that these voices are lying, and I declare my purpose. It's also one of my daily affirmations that I use to set my intention each morning.

Finding your purpose is a crucial part of living a fulfilling life. When you are living on purpose, everything flows smoothly and opportunities arise all around you. When you start to live away from your purpose, though, it becomes harder to get things going and you start to have more bad luck. These are the subtle red flags life gives you to let you know that you are off course; it's up to you to listen and take the next steps.

Another step in my healing journey was recognizing that in the last fifteen years, I have lost a brother, a sister, my father, aunts, uncles, cousins, and all of my grandparents except one – it was a huge transitional phase in my life. Grief is such a difficult rollercoaster of a ride, especially when your foundation has been shaken so hard that you feel unstable. I was a single mother barely making it through each day, and at every turn it seemed my mentors and pillars in life were leaving this earth. Through these losses, I found strength in realizing how precious and fragile life is and learned to love the ones who are still here with me even harder. It was also a reminder that we all arrived here with our life plans, and that leaving is part of the "contract." Each person left because their purpose on Earth was fulfilled, and so it was time to go. Everyone in the world is grieving something, and everyone goes through the phases of grief and transition differently. So, remember that we need to show love to each other, and to yourself.

I have one grandparent left, my grandmother Mildred. She is ninety-two years old, and she is my hero. I have been learning our culture and traditions from her over my lifetime, and she has displayed an incredible amount of strength and stamina during every single one of her teachings. As I watched her one day, I realized that there will come a time when I will be the elder, the knowledge keeper. I will be the oldest person in my family, and everybody older than me will have left this earth for the spirit world. This is the reality of the circle of life. Ever since, I constantly remind myself to cherish the moments with my family and to make amazing memories with them. My goal is to have a full, long life and maintain a youthful mindset, just like my grandmother has.

Over the years, I have learned that what's important in life is love, family, your peace, your happiness, and your time. Some people believe it's fame, fortune, success in business, or material items, but do those truly bring you happiness and peace? When your time comes to transition from Earth into the spirit world, will you be thinking about the raise you got? Your jobs? The items you bought? No, you will be thinking of your family, your time, your love, and your adventures. Relationships have a great impact on your wellbeing and happiness, especially your relationship with yourself, so make sure you are nurturing them. I want to die with memories, not dreams.

All of these lessons have come to a head in my current

relationship. Eleven years ago, I was re-introduced to Lennard, a man I had met many years before at a conference about the mountain pine beetle epidemic our province was soon to endure. At the time, we were both in the process of getting divorced, and we both had two children. As a result, we found that being able to truly fall in love was one of the hardest things we had to do. This may sound contradictory at first, but let me explain. We had both been hurt during our relationships in life, and when our hearts are hurt, we start to put walls up to protect ourselves from being hurt again. So, both Lennard and I had to work on taking these walls down to expose our raw, authentic, true selves. We had to take a good look at ourselves in this state, feel the feelings we had locked up, and let the hurts go so we could heal. We stopped self-sabotaging ourselves and protecting our hearts and let each other in. Doing this by ourselves probably would have been easier – our timing was out of sync, so the process took a lot of patience and honesty on both sides – but we got through it together. After four years we had our daughter, after five years we moved in together, after six years we bought a house, and after eight years we eloped and got married in Maui. If you think about it, we did it the opposite of what society tells us we should do with our lives, and that's more than okay! The only things that matters is that we are happy.

Learning to love and let love in was one of life's hardest lessons, and yet it was also the most rewarding. Today, Lennard and I are truly head over heels in love with each other, and our love grows stronger and stronger every day. To achieve this, we stay aware of what's going on around us, within us, and with us, and we respect each other's space, needs, and – our greatest asset – time. We also strive to keep our wheel of life balanced, which includes:

- Family relationships/significant other
- Career, contributions, and the unique gifts we bring to the world
- Personal improvements, skills, and education
- Our life purpose
- Community relations
- Physical health and activities
- Mental health and activities
- Emotional health and activities
- Spiritual health and activities
- Finances
- Living environment
- Adventures, creativity, hobbies, vacations, and rest

Finding and maintaining this balance will help you lead a healthy and fulfilling life, but it is an ongoing lifelong process. Lennard and I constantly do check-ins with ourselves to see if we are balanced. For instance, we will rate our work life, our relationships, and our family on a scale of one to ten, with one being very unhealthy and ten being very healthy. Sometimes we are so focused on one part of our life that the other parts fall behind, so it is important to assess all of these areas. After every check in, we may set some goals to realign ourselves and find that balance once more.

As I stand on top of the "hill" with all these life lessons under my belt and look towards the future, I've started to think about what I want to achieve in the years to come. For one, I've realized that I should be travelling when I am young! I don't want to wait until I retire because there are things I want to do while I am still physically strong, such as hiking through France, Italy, and Switzerland. I have already travelled to quite a few places, and I want to continue exploring this passion on an annual basis. My goal is to try and go to a new place every year. This is an achievable goal for me because I can simply go somewhere new in the area I live, or I can go to a different continent – whatever is within my reach at that time.

Another life goal is to stay as healthy as possible – not only physically but also spiritually, emotionally, and mentally. To achieve this, I will use the teachings from the medicine wheel to keep my life in balance. This includes physical, spiritual, emotional, and mental self-care; some examples of each of these can be found below. By practicing self-care in all of these areas, I strive to keep the balance between all four realms.

- Physical self-care: exercising, eating healthy food, drinking enough water, getting adequate sleep and rest
- Spiritual self-care: meditation, spending time out in nature, doing something nice for someone else
- Emotional self-care: setting healthy boundaries, spending time with loved ones
- Mental self-care: positive affirmations, blocking out media and social media, practicing mindfulness, seeing a counsellor

No matter how hard we work at achieving this balance, life happens and negative situations arise. The key to moving through and past these events is being aware and honest with yourself and having healthy coping skills. This may include playing sports, hiking, painting, scrapbooking, getting together with a supportive group of friends, going for a spa day, or anything that has a positive impact on your life. We are all human, with human feelings and human needs. It's okay to not be okay at times, but don't stay there. Do your check-ins and set achievable goals that will bring you closer to what you want in life. A vision board is a great way to guide yourself through the process of thinking about and manifesting what you want in life, and will help you focus on your goals.

Every year we make a trip around the sun, and every year we can make the next trip be our best one yet. It's up to you to take control of your life and be accountable for your decisions and the consequences that come with them. So, find your balance and your life purpose and set your eyes on the incredible journey you have ahead of you, because the best is yet to come.

About Kristy Henkes-Joe

Kristy is a strong, passionate, independent woman from the Dakelh (Carrier) Tribe from the central interior of BC. Kristy spent her childhood years in the Tl'azt'en and Nak'azdli Nation with a large family that immersed itself in the harvesting and cultural activities within the family's Keyoh (territory). Today she calls Merritt, BC home and is married to her husband Lennard Joe, who is from the Shackan Band within the Nlaka'pamux Nation, and together they have raised five children.

Kristy's healing journey has given her the strength and perspective to live life in a good way and to fulfill her purpose, which is to lead others to reach their full potential so they will find peace, love, and happiness within. She has played an integral part in the healing journey of many Indigenous youth, elders, women, men, and organizations throughout British Columbia. Her innovative and dynamic attitude, along with her strong administrative background, has allowed her to excel as an orchestrator and implementor of many programs to create stronger, healthier, and safer communities. She is recognized and acknowledged by many chiefs and leaders throughout the province for her tireless commitment to creating a healthier and happier nation.

Email: kristyannjoe@hotmail.com
Facebook: Kristy Henkes-Joe
Twitter: @KristyHenkesJoe
Instagram: kristy_henkesjoe

10

Just Say Yes!

by Amy Hadikin

*"A candle does not need to burn out its flame
in order to light another.
In fact, it can light limitless candles."*
Author Unknown

Just Say Yes!

By Amy Hadikin

Recently, I found myself wondering how I got here – how I began living my passions and dreams. My life hasn't always been easy, but something changed along the way and I now live a life I once only dreamed of. After some thought, I realized it started when I stopped overthinking and just started saying yes to my passions. Want a gym? Yes! Want a restaurant? Yes! Want a yoga studio too? Yes! Want financial freedom? YES!

It all started with a much simpler step than that though, and that is when I said yes to ME. Two and a half years ago, I left a toxic relationship in which I had put my life and dreams on hold in order to take care of my man and family. Throughout this relationship, I had started to dislike myself more and more as I diminished my character by doing what everyone else wanted. But when my mom died from five different cancers at the young age of sixty-six, I'd finally had enough. I didn't want to die early like my mom, so I started saying "yes" to me.

Unfortunately, just saying yes wasn't enough. It took another two years of misery in that relationship, with my depression getting worse and worse every day, before I gathered my power – along with my child, the two cutest puppies ever, my car, some clothes, and of course my Vitamix – and got out. I didn't know how things were going to turn out, but I knew I needed out of that environment. I recently heard a quote that explains how I felt in that moment: "You can't heal in the same environment where you got sick." Thankfully, I was able to bounce back to my best self because of my healthy lifestyle, which I had already been leading for years prior to this relationship – although it had fallen to the wayside as I had prioritized other people over myself.

I had decided to make a change to my lifestyle back in the early 2000s, when I was thirty years old. I had come down with a dis-ease, and spent about a year struggling to figure out what was happening to me. Eventually, I found out that I had a common condition called gastric reflux disease, and that it was completely manageable – all I had to do was take a pill for the rest of my life. NO WAY! I was only thirty, and I was NOT going to go on a medication for years and years. I knew there had to be a better option.

I researched alternative methods of promoting health, which was against the norm at that time, and in the process I found the book *Raw Family: A True Story of Awakening* by the Boutenko family. After reading the book, I went on to see the family speak at a local lecture. They shared their story of how they changed their lives and rid themselves of their diseases through a raw vegan diet. Sergei, the father, had a tumor in his throat the size of a tennis ball and was able to heal himself through a raw food lifestyle. The children in the family graduated from high school three to four years earlier than other kids their age, and I believe the same went for college – the clarity of a clean diet helped them immensely. As someone who had been a junk food vegetarian for the past decade, I said YES, I want that! I did my best to live a raw vegan lifestyle from that day forward, and I was able to almost instantly get rid of my so-called "lifelong disease."

I truly believe that I have only had the power and the opportunities to live my best life because of my vegan lifestyle – or, at the very least, that it has allowed me to recognize and act upon the opportunities available to me. Throughout all the chaos and uncertainty in life, my clean eating – along with my active lifestyle – was the one constant that got me through every challenge that came my way. Clean eating has helped keep my body as healthy as possible, while activities and sports have kept me focused, taught me how to work with a team, and kept me out of trouble.

I have an undeniable urge to help people excel and succeed in life, so after seeing the benefits of this lifestyle for myself, I wanted to pass it on to the people I love. My daughter, Maya, came into this world when I was thirty-two, and her dad and I raised her as a raw vegan until she was four and a half years old. As a result, she was a strong, dynamic, smart child who rarely got sick. And then came the school system. When Maya began attending school, we were given a strict list of foods that were not allowed, including chocolate and nuts. I tried to explain to them that my child was a raw vegan, which meant that nuts were a staple in her diet and her "treats" were raw vegan chocolate. Unfortunately, I was unable to keep up with arguing with "the norm," and my child started a typical SAD (Standard American Diet). There were immediate and noticeable changes in her behaviour, especially when it came to focus, and her strong will turned into stubbornness. I will say that she still has a wicked immune system, though, thanks to her amazing start in life.

Maya is fourteen years old at the time of writing this, and she is very strong, independent, and determined. She will make choices that resonate with her, and I fully accept that. I have not yet gotten her off of the SAD diet, but she does now ask for a green juice and raw caesar salad every morning. So, I have made putting this together a part of my daily routine. When and if she chooses to come back to the raw and/or vegan lifestyle, I will be there for her.

Coming back to my story ... I first said yes to a healthy lifestyle, and then I said yes to myself and struck out on my own. However, it didn't take long for me to realize that I now only had myself to rely on. I had to figure out how I would get out of bed each day, provide for my child, and make myself happy. I tried and tried to enjoy my career as a realtor, which I had been doing for twelve years, but it just didn't click anymore. Yes, we needed money, but that couldn't be my only motivation. Up until then, I got what I wanted by pushing and pushing, feeling like I was walking uphill with a fifty-pound backpack, and I was finally realizing that life should be easy and enjoyable. My alignment was out of whack, and I needed to get it back on track.

During moments of silence and meditation, I kept asking the universe what my purpose was. Life can't just be about the daily grind. In an effort to bring enjoyment back into my life, I made a conscious decision to only do things I love. I got back to working out. I only allowed people in my life who were good for my mental health and who enhanced my life in some way or another. I stopped looking and searching and decided to "just be." I knew my passions were in the health and wellness field, I just didn't know how that would manifest. I figured that if I simply kept filling my plate with goodness, it would all work out – at least, that's what I hoped.

I did have one dream in the back of my mind: for years and years, I had wanted to create a retreat called Changes that would incorporate fitness, clean eating, and personal empowerment. It would be a one-stop wellness shop where people could come and get their life in alignment; a Disneyland for people who needed change. I wrote this dream down in numerous journals, desired it, wished for it. Then, one magical day, a gym was offered to me for sale! I said YES, I wanted to buy the gym. I didn't know where the time or money would come from, but I still jumped in with both feet and purchased it with my sister. Part of my lifelong vision was now coming to fruition! Although my heart was no longer in the corporate world, I struggled through anyways so I could fund my passion. For the next year, I attempted to still work as a realtor AND get back into health and wellness.

However, I guess the universe really wanted me out of the corporate world and living to my fullest potential. My mom, my sister and I had started a restaurant back in 2008 and sold it in 2011. Now, eight years later, I was given the option to buy it back. I said no at first as time and money were still a concern. However, when I was in Hawaii on my annual bestie birthday trip, I was given some quite obvious signs to say yes. One of the biggest signs came when my bestie and I were swimming and talking about whether or not I should purchase the restaurant. Then, as we were chatting, a big, beautiful sea turtle swam below me. Sea turtles often symbolize patience, wisdom, endurance, and good luck, so as soon as we saw it, we looked at each other and said yes! After making sure that my daughter was okay with me putting in so much time to a new business venture, I decided to just jump in and figure it out as I went. And with that, two pieces of my vision were now active. Yes, I eventually wanted both fitness and clean eating under one roof, but this was a good start.

At the same time I decided to buy the restaurant, the universe came knocking again. "What now, Universe?" I asked. The answer was my truest passion: hot yoga. I had paid for my teacher training about four years ago, but I hadn't been able to get away from my family and the corporate world for the thirty-day certification. I kept postponing and postponing, but then I learned during my trip to Hawaii that my teacher trainer, who normally taught all over the world, would be in my town. I had a gym with a hot room, and I had two months to spare before I took over the restaurant. I reached out to the training school and was told that if I could find some more students, they would run a program at my gym and work it around my schedule. Yes!

At this point, I was now juggling the gym, my real estate career, the preparations for the restaurant takeover, and my hot yoga teacher training. Thankfully, due to my clean eating, my regular meditation, and my workouts, I had the energy I needed to keep moving forward.

As I looked towards what would happen after I completed my yoga teacher training, I realised I needed to make another change. The current building for our gym had a tiny, tiny yoga room – not quite my vision. Well, our lease was up and we needed to move, so my sister and I decided to find a new place that better suited our needs. We found a great location for the gym with high visibility, but it still had no room for a yoga studio. Despite this issue, we decided to get moved in and figure out the rest later. Once again, the universe stepped in.

Immediately after we signed the lease for the new location, the perfect place for a yoga studio opened up in the same complex. Yes, yes, yes! Now that I was working on living my life in alignment with my passions, everything was falling into place.

Two months later the gym was moved, the yoga studio was under renovation, and the restaurant was ready for me to take over, all while I was still maintaining my career as a realtor. Of course, time was still a concern. How could I fit everything in? I knew I could do it all, but did I want to? I had been burning the candle at both ends for months, and I decided that something had to change. In moments like this, I always look at my life and say, "Amy, if you won the lottery, what would you do?" And as I sat in silence and asked myself that question, the answer became clear: I would stay on my health and wellness path. The healthier I get, the healthier my family gets and the more I can change lives for the better. I would still own the gym and the yoga studio, teach hot yoga, and run and enhance the restaurant. What I needed to do was let my safety blanket go and fully give up my job in the corporate world. Decision made! It took me a couple months to pull the trigger, but at the time I am writing this, I can proudly say that I am 100% fully committed to my health and wellness path, and to helping people live their best lives by finding their true, authentic purpose.

However, there were still more changes ahead. Recently, I had a dear friend ask me, "If in this moment, it wasn't for fear, what would you do?" She told me that I was spreading myself too thin, and that I needed to figure out where ALL my passion was leading me. I meditated on this and came to the conclusion to sell my restaurant and put all my focus into yoga. I truly care about the people around me and want everyone to be their best selves, and the yoga studio is where

I am best able to do that. I can help others and influence their lives by teaching all the programs that I love, like mom-and-tot yoga, senior yoga, rainbow yoga, and so much more. I am also getting back to my vegan lifestyle coaching, where I provide in-home consultations as well as lessons at the yoga studio on how to create a lifestyle that allows you to be in peace everyday. However, I am still proud of what I accomplished in my time owning the restaurant – I have transitioned it into a thriving vegan restaurant where the atmosphere is awesome and the food is amazing.

Every day I hear questions like "How do you do it?" and "Where do you get your energy?" My answer every single time is a clean, vegan diet and living my passions. I have stayed consistent with my diet and lifestyle for many years, and I wouldn't be where I am today without it. Don't get me wrong, I still "cheat" and eat "bad" vegan food. But when I do, I notice that my life is not so easy to navigate. I don't feel my best, and I lack energy. I feel out of alignment. When I stick to a clean lifestyle, though, I feel amazing, vibrant, dynamic, and empowered. I have navigated some very tough obstacles and had to figure things out, but I believe in living with passion and purpose, and I will always continue to grow.

I would like to share a few tips to get you on YOUR path of alignment and purpose, and it starts with asking yourself what you would do with your life if you won the lottery. And once you have your answer, do that! Watch some documentaries, listen to some YouTube, read books, do whatever you need to do in order to find a way to achieve your dreams. Then, once you've found your direction, set your sails and head off. Where your eyes go, your body will follow. Nothing happens instantly, though, so you need to listen and watch for signs.

As you go on this journey, it is important to surround

yourself with people who will support you. One of my biggest lessons was learning the importance of my circle. Who will be there in the good times and the bad? Who would be the first person I called with great news, and with not so good news? Ask yourself those same questions, and then spend your time with those people.

Finally, do only what YOU love. As my story has shown, once you begin following your passions and living in alignment, the universe will provide what you need to achieve your dreams. So, find what makes you happy, keep an eye out for the opportunities to pursue it, and when you find them – or more often, when they find you – just say yes!

About Amy Hadikin

Amy Hadikin is dynamic and passionate about living her best life. She loves helping others and is dedicated to improving quality of life for all. After getting out of a non-serving relationship and life, Amy said yes to all her passions that were knocking at her door.

Today, Amy finally lives her truest purpose by helping others to live their best life in the yoga studio and through vegan lifestyle coaching and meditation. Her focus is being a strong role model for Maya, her beautiful daughter, and to instill in her that she, along with everyone else in life, should not just survive but THRIVE.

Want to learn more? Join Amy on her Facebook page every Monday at 8:00 p.m. Pacific time for a FREE live broadcast. During these fifteen-minute sessions, she addresses the questions that people ask her on a regular basis, and provides constant motivation.

Facebook: AskAmyH

11

Pause. Breathe. Shift.

by Tammy Scarlett

"Your task is not to seek for love, but merely to seek and find all the barriers within yourself that you have built against it."
Rumi

Pause. Breathe. Shift.

By Tammy Scarlett

In 2012, my husband left and my family dissolved. It was always going to be a painful time regardless of the circumstances, but I was ill-prepared even though I knew it was coming. Our relationship ended with the greatest loss and grief imaginable, and the ensuing stress and despair brought about a chain of events that have led me to where I am today. The learning and growing I gained during this time, as well as the self-discovery and awareness of that loss of love and way of life, prepared me for what is and what will be as I continue to move forward.

I credit the breakup of my marriage, as horrible as it seemed at the time, with the saving of myself, my life, and perhaps my very soul. I was an empath with unhealthy boundaries, all of which had been breached at some point. I was unsure of myself and afraid to make mistakes. Messing up meant disappointing someone, and as an empath, *that* feels really bad. Disillusioned by the façade I had created, I had never really been open and honest with ANYONE, myself included. This denial, along with letting my ego overwhelm me, was blocking my self-love. I lived on the edge, defending the perimeter to avoid looking inward, suppressing emotions, hiding abuses, accepting lies, giving away my power, and avoiding confrontation at all cost out of a fear of rejection and abandonment. I allowed myself to be absorbed by the people around me, and so everything I valued disappeared. It was the only way I knew how to feel safe, useful, and seen. All of this meant I had cultured my persona in an effort to protect myself. I had morphed into who I believed I was expected to be, mimicking qualities of those around me as I tried to piece together the person I needed to be in order to survive, to succeed, and to be loved. I had taken from others and given away all I had. "I" was lost.

During the turmoil of the last days of my marriage, I began to look for ways to save us – but, in the end, I saved myself. I read *Real Love* by Greg Baer as part of this process, and it gave me the ability to shift my perspective – an ability I hold in the highest regard. It led me to have a deeper understanding of compassion and to have empathy and forgiveness for myself. It also showed me that being honest with myself was one of the keys to happiness. Through this book, I came to understand that we forge a prison out of our past traumas and experiences in order to protect ourselves from hurts and dramas, and I had built those walls up so high that I couldn't see the way out. But the key to freedom had always been in my own pocket, and that key was recognizing I needed to address my negative beliefs about myself, assess my habits, and notice the patterns that kept replaying in my life – ones of co-dependency, waiting to be saved, hiding traumas, giving away my power to keep the peace, and operating from a victim mentality. When we know better, we can do better.

I was on an empowering path but by the year after the divorce, my previous condition of ruin had manifested in my physical body in the form of breast cancer. Energetically speaking, the breast was the natural place for dis-ease to appear within me. Besides all the physical connections the breast has to the body – acting as part of the lymphatic system, feeding babies, stimulating the uterus, providing sexual pleasure, and more – it has many unseen functions as well. It is a source of feminine prowess, an object of ridicule, an instrument of abuse, and for me, a gauge of my self-worth. I had always been small-chested, and this had been a source of much derision throughout my life. In my younger years, I was even told very loudly in a public place that I could be a model if I only had some boobs.

The official diagnosis was triple negative invasive ductal carcinoma, a rare and aggressive form of breast cancer with lymph node involvement. I was told I would need a mastectomy. The cancer was only in the right side but, due to the nature of this disease, I opted to have the left removed too as a precaution. The initial surgery included the removal of my breasts and the placement of tissue expanders, which would be filled once a week before the treatments began. Then it was on to chemo and radiation before they could do the implant exchange, which took place in June 2014. The decision to get implants is one that I went into blindly and for the wrong reasons. My husband had been a "boob man," and I was still reeling from the impending divorce and wished to hurt him. In reality, though, I was only harming myself. Little did I know that the textured implants provided for reconstruction after cancer had only been approved in 2013, and they had been flagged by the FDA for their potential to cause cancer in 2011. I was not told of the risks, though, so I willingly accepted these ticking time bombs.

As I worked on healing my physical body, I also worked on healing my mental and emotional state. After my treatment, I had taken on the task of becoming a certified life coach. The learning was a welcome distraction from the dramatic demise of my relationship – it helped me focus on a purpose, and on learning something that could potentially help others. With the new knowledge that came from the certification process, I started listening to the conversations I was carrying on in my mind, and I found them to be disturbing. "You're flawed." "You are too sensitive." "You don't deserve that." You get the picture. These stories had been on repeat my entire lifetime, and I was shocked by how cruel they were. Why were they so harsh? I was a nice person, wasn't I? I had many friends, didn't I? But as I sat with these thoughts, I realized that I didn't trust any of these friends – and more importantly, that I didn't even trust myself. This was a revelation. How could I trust others if I couldn't trust myself? Did I actually know *how* to trust someone? When was the last time I completely trusted ANYONE? If I wanted answers to these questions, I'd have to go back to the root cause – that first instance where the behaviour was utilized to "get something" or as a "protection" from something. When we can recognize and understand the motive behind our actions, we can begin to forgive ourselves and/or forgive others.

With some personal growth work, the masks I was hiding behind disappeared, leaving me naked and exposed, tired and distraught, broken and ashamed. I thought this was the end, that my life was over, and it was. But it was also the beginning of a new cycle, a new way, and a new me. This would be the real me that steps up and tackles any challenge given. This would be the me that I was meant to be.

We must save ourselves in order to continue forward on a new path – one that takes us towards a purpose that is truer to who we are. The trick is to become response-able; the catch is that we need to get to a place of awareness about ourselves and our behaviours. When we are ignorant and unaware, we operate from a place of reaction, protection, and manipulation. These old habits are based on learned experiences of what has worked in the past, but for whatever reason, they eventually stop working.

One practice that helped me become response-able was a program I developed called 50~50 – a yoga-like, self-regulated, trauma-guided, intuitive program. When I was diagnosed in 2013, I became aware of how disconnected I was from my body. It was numb; *I* was numb. Through this practice, I was able to get back in tune with my body and self – a reconnection of sorts. This practice incorporates generational work, appreciation for physical being-ness, and self-love. It requires me to be honest with myself about myself; to become response-able, and to take full responsibility for me.

I am grateful that I took this time to work on myself, because all of these new skills were about to be put to the test. In July 2018, I went in for a meet-and-greet appointment with my new doctor after moving cities. There wasn't much for us to discuss as I was very healthy and thriving, but I did mention that I was experiencing some discomfort in my breasts. The doctor informed me she suspected I had capsular contracture, which is when the collagen-fiber scar tissue capsule contracts around the implant as your body defends itself from the foreign object. She set up an appointment with a plastic surgeon to address the issue before the implant could rupture. Around this time, I had heard about some problems people were having with their implants, but I hadn't given them much thought. There was little awareness of breast implant illness (BII), breast implant-associated anaplastic large cell lymphoma (BIA-ALCL) or silicone reactivity disorder. I had started to notice some fatigue in my day-to-day life, but I didn't suspect the implants could be the cause.

Unfortunately, the capsule containing the implant burst in January 2019, before I could get in to see the plastic surgeon. To understand why this is a problem, imagine a rock coated with sand (the textured implant) that is put inside a zip-top sandwich bag filled with toxic soup (the capsule). Now, imagine squeezing the bag. At first there is a little give, but eventually the bag opens and the fluid exits. The rock still appears intact, but perhaps some sand has come off the rock and floods out with the toxic fluid. These substances and their effects on the body are still a mystery, and the potential conditions they can cause have a long list of symptoms. The only known remedy at this time is removal of the implant.

By the time my capsule ruptured, these issues were becoming mainstream media stories. Anyone who had received an implant, especially a textured implant, was susceptible. There were FDA hearings, product recalls, and panic. Plastic surgeons and physicians were scrambling to serve their patients while also protecting their practise. There was limited research on the subject, leaving doctors at a loss. This is a nightmare for patients who go in seeking answers only to be met by the proverbial deer in the headlights. Are they afraid to diagnose, or do they just have no answers? Some may be worried about repercussions, but others might prefer to remain in the dark. I never imagined I'd be on the forefront of such an issue, but I was experiencing concerning symptoms and wanted to get testing done to figure out exactly what was wrong. Unfortunately, getting any answers was a long and frustrating process. It's unsettling as a patient to have to do your own research and convey this information to the health authorities, only to be met by a blank stare, a bruised ego, or resistance. To them I am just another person in their office, but to me, this is my life.

Enduring pain is one thing, but going through unnecessary mental anguish is another. People shouldn't have to wait so long to be reassured; tests should just be done as requested. It took nine months for the oncologist to tell me that my cancer had not returned, and that I had no signs of lymphoma. Waiting for a nay or yay from a cancer doctor is a nerve-wracking thing, especially after having already had cancer, so changes need to be made to make this process faster, easier, and less painful.

After my rupture, the one thing that was certain was that my implants needed to be removed as soon as possible. I was about to lose my breasts for good; this time, there will be no reconstruction. This time, I'd let them go graciously. Though I'd had them for only a short time, I did get to glimpse the spells they cast on others – ones of jealousy, desire, lust, and prudishness. However, breasts do not make a woman. As I returned to my original athletic body type, I realized that my inner beauty is what I put forward. When I present myself, it is the essence of me that comes through. Today, I prepare my appearance to the best of my ability, working with what I have. I dress in what I like, put on make-up or not, style my hair or not, check my teeth, smile, and never look back. I have come to value the person I am without the trappings of the outer shell.

In my mind, I'd thought I would have the surgery, heal, and get on with my life. Well, I had the surgery in March 2019, but the rest I'm still working on. While I had prepared for the loss of my breasts and the subsequent recovery from the explant, I hadn't expected other changes and symptoms to persist. My left arm and hand feel like they belong to someone else due to pain and numbness – collateral damage from the surgery. I also continuously lose my train of thought as a result of the leftover brain fog from the "poisoning" that came with the ruptured implant capsule. I am easily distracted and find it hard to stay focused for long periods. Though I am familiar with healing, this latest trauma has been kicking my ass. Not to worry, though, because I kick back!

As I have travelled down this path, I have been guided towards a greater purpose. The stumbles and adjustments along the way have helped me to narrow the path, to leave the things that didn't work behind, and to move forward, even if it's a different direction than I had expected. And this path has led me towards making the most of what IS, like writing this chapter to share my story. It also led me to another way of sharing and being in service.

In 2015, after the required year post-treatment waiting period, I began volunteering at the cancer centre helping with chemo-teach and relaxation therapy groups as well as acting as a chemo room support person. I had used the services at this centre during my own treatment, and I always knew that I would return to give back. I'd hoped to encourage other patients, to ease their suffering in any manner possible, and to assist the care staff. I wanted to be hands-on. So, in the time leading up to my volunteering, I began gathering information and paying close attention to the things that could be of value. I had already completed two levels of therapeutic touch, and I soon discovered integrated energy healing, which involves re-patterning the client's biofield, reading physical structures, assisting in the release of traumatic experience, and building resilience. After receiving a timely payout from the divorce, I invested in myself and enrolled to become an advanced integrated energy healing (AIEH) practitioner while continuing to look for useful ways to help others, make contacts, gather resources, and source out readily-available, ethical, organic, local products that may be beneficial during the healing processes.

Currently, I am unable to continue with my AIEH studies and I'm not well enough physically to engage in a "regular" workplace role. However, this has given me the opportunity to focus on utilizing my unique personal history, skillset, and experiences to make a difference in the world. Through potential sponsors and donations, the divorce payout, fundraising, online proceeds from the Shift Shop, and a "pay it forward" option, I have been developing Souls Shift Wellness, a not-for-profit outreach foundation that will offer co-creative retreats and workshops to newly diagnosed breast cancer patients in British Columbia. The retreats and workshops will gift these women with an interactive experience and provide them with some practical tips and coping skills, along with helping them access other helpful resources that may assist in their journey. These could potentially help women with other breast-related issues as well, such as explant surgeries, breast implant illness, breast and other cancers, pretty much any woman with or without breasts! Soul Shift Wellness will help women like me become better, not bitter. It will help them move out of victimhood and into wellness by creating a chain of positive reactions, softening the blows of devastating losses, and bridging the communication gaps between women and the medical community as well as within the medical community itself.

I have faced many challenges as I have moved through this journey, and it has taken great effort and some serious personal growth to overcome them. I'm reminded of the saying, "The definition of insanity is doing the same thing over and over again and expecting a different result." Today, I recognize the patterns in my behaviour and take steps to change them. Instead of saying "why is this happening to me," I instead ask "what can I learn from this?"

Living in my truth has set me free – free to be my authentic self, to make my own choices, and to strive towards positive change. Being honest with myself allows me to see/call my own bullshit, recognize my own resistances, and cultivate compassion and kindness through self-love. Being fully present of the mind/body connection helps me notice health issues sooner, while having awareness of my habitual reactions to negative triggers helps me restructure them. This is a trial-and-error process, and it's okay to have missteps along the way. When I slip, I forgive, and then I continue forward, cultivating patience through perseverance

Another important aspect of my healing journey has been changing my definition of hope. For me, hope used to be a fear-controlled anxiety trigger. Because of the unknown outcomes, the loss of control, and the uncertainty of having a desired destination but no direction, hope was only a "maybe" during the challenging times in my life. I have since changed that trigger by redefining HOPE as "Honouring Our Perceived Expectations." I have worked on letting go of the future result and surrendering to the open-endedness of the future – on releasing control and letting go of fear through gratitude and love. I allow myself to have hope without being attached to what I am hoping for, believing in the higher good and the potentiality of the most positive outcome.

To those of you who recognize yourself in some of this chapter – those who are facing adversities and feel lost, afraid, and unsure of what to do next – I hope my story has shown you the importance of moving forward and taking any step, even the smallest one, to change the current situation. No matter how bleak things may look, there is always hope; you just need to pause, breathe, and shift.

About Tammy Scarlett

Tammy Scarlett is in love with the person she's fought to become. Presently recovering from explant surgery on the heels of breast cancer and divorce, the release of her soul came with the stripping away of body and mind to discover the heart of a compassionate warrior. She strives to be a powerful role model for her two children, Makenzie and Seth.

Tammy has served as a volunteer in many capacities, including at the North Fraser Therapeutic Riding Association, Circle F Horse Rescue, and the BC Cancer Agency. Her recent pursuits include a life coaching certification, studies in trauma and strategic resilience, and becoming an integrative energy healing practitioner. She also sits on the board of a developing charity for restorative tattooing, After Cancer Art.

Now, a fresh start has come after facing her own mortality. Learning to let go created space for new possibilities. Through her extensive lived experience, Tammy has been called to be a healer and dedicates her time to building something of consequence. Upon being released as a cancer patient, she immediately began creating Soul Shift Wellness, a non-profit foundation designed to support women with breast cancer.

www.soulshiftwellness.com
Email: theshiftwork@gmail.com

12

Change – It's What We Do

by Jocelyn Johnston

*"My fault, my failure, is not in the passions I have,
but in my lack of control of them."*
Jack Kerouak

Change – It's What We Do

By Jocelyn Johnston

Because of the way it plays with our hormones, menopause impacts our brains as well as our bodies – and it sure messed with mine for awhile. As the amounts of estrogen and progesterone fluctuate, we are taken on a ride we would never board if it weren't for "the change." No one told me I could never actually plan my life, or that I would fly through so many chapters, but I am telling you now that we change. We are *supposed* to change. No good can come from fighting it.

Over the years, I have come to understand that hormonal fluctuations didn't just warn me when things were about to change, they were the agents of change. In chatting with other women, I have since discovered this to be true for many of us. For better or for worse, hormones are responsible for so much of what goes on in our lives, starting from when we are quite young.

My first experience with losing control over my mind and body was just prior to my first period. I was still a child when I found myself attracted to boys. Certain that I was the only person in the world who wanted to kiss a boy, I worked hard to hide my desires from my mother. She had two older daughters, and maybe that was why we never spoke about such things. I assume she had talked with my older sisters and, with a growing family and issues of her own, believed she had done her bit. So, when the physical aspect of my menses arrived in addition to the emotional part, it was unexpected, messy, embarrassing, and even frightening. I felt that I was no longer my mother's sweet, innocent "little" girl, and since I didn't want to disappoint her, I chose to tell her nothing. Instead, feeling quite alone and warrior-like, I left home.

I kissed a few boys after that and believed I had things pretty much figured out when I got pregnant – three times in three years. Now there were new feelings to hide. I knew where babies came from, but I didn't know that there was more to growing a child in your body than getting fat. I also grew hips, a mustache, and stretch marks. I was emotional, cranky, and horny, and when the day finally arrived, the labour pains were so severe that I believed I was dying. With no one to help, no quality sleep, back pain, and hemorrhoids for years after my first was born, I still can't believe I went on to have two more children, and so close together. The biological drive to procreate – to create chaos in my life – was ridiculously, irresponsibly irresistible.

Looking back over those years, I realize I struggled largely because I believed I was alone in my humanity. If I had actually trusted myself; if I had not been in such a hurry to be an adult and prove that I was strong, independent, and could do everything on my own; if I'd had someone to talk to; then maybe I would have done things a little differently.

The only thing I really regretted was not finishing school – not even high school. I had wanted to be a teacher but instead, at twenty-three years old, I found myself the mother of three boys, living on my in-laws' property in an old house with rats and bears and no heat or water. I had talked myself into thinking that would be cool. It wasn't. I did everything I could to make that place a home as my world expanded with the arrival of each child. I did everything I could for my kids, but I knew it wasn't enough. I was certain that I was a failure, and that this was how things would be forever.

But things change. The hormones quieted down, and once the boys started school, a new chapter revealed itself. I started nesting again – this time, for my own future. I enrolled in a distance course here and there, and by the time my kids graduated high school, I was delighted to discover that I too had enough credits to graduate with a degree in education.

Things were looking good, but then they changed once again. I was forty when my oldest made me a grandma, and I could almost feel those first pre-perimenopause hormones begin to seep into my life. Seeing this tiny new life reminded me that we all have an expiry date, and my body started to whisper something about how I shouldn't get too comfortable just yet.

Pre-perimenopause is not something I just made up; it's something I lived. Most women take this time to re-evaluate their lives. Without small children to concern ourselves with, we can more easily leave abusive relationships, or even just ones that are no longer working. I have met women who were finally able to stop denying their sexual preference and begin a new life with a new wife. Some were able to take a "time-out" and go on an adventure, returning home at the end of it, while others never came back. Some women rediscovered their own partner, fell in love again, and moved into retirement, adding a new layer to the relationship and the life they built together. My mother called it a "mid-life crisis," looking down her nose at people who bought sports cars or got perms. But just because she didn't believe in it, didn't make it any less real. My mother just called it "golf." She spent her days with her tribe at the golf course, and she was happy.

I hated golf, so my experience with this time of life went a little differently. My husband was busy with his work, as he had been our whole married life, so I spent a lot of time on my own. I earned a master's degree just to stay busy. When I tried to find work locally there was nothing available, so I began to take jobs where I could be home on the weekend. Then I took ones further afield, returning home when I could. My world began to expand yet again, from mom and wife to teacher and co-worker. I wasn't the same person at forty-five that I had been at thirty. I had changed, and my husband didn't like it. He *accused* me of changing and said there was no need for it – that he would "take care of me." His words made me realize that if things were going to change, it was up to me to change them.

I left him when I was forty-eight. I wasn't running away from anything; I was running toward my own life. Leaving him, along with my home of over twenty-five years, was the hardest, most painful thing I had ever done, but it was what I needed to do. I knew it was going to be hard to stay away, so I took a teaching position in the Middle East – somewhere so far away that it would be almost impossible for me to change my mind.

In the little Sultanate of Oman, my world expanded from largely just my family to include people from all over the world. I found myself among Arabs and Indians, Europeans and Egyptians. I had read stories of Sinbad, but now I found myself walking in his footsteps. It was a magical adventure. I taught young men who wore white robes and little caps and found they were no different than my own boys. I felt proud to be Canadian but discovered that I loved Oman as well. I no longer felt limited by political borders, so I was ready to become an Australian resident when the time came, and later a Mexican one. I discovered the world to be made up of people, not nationalities.

Life in Oman put me on a steep learning curve, and while it was fun and exciting, it was by no means "better" than life at home. I wouldn't have had the strength to stay if I hadn't found romance – a crazy relationship with an Australian named Yasin that should have lasted just a year as we had little in common, but that I clung to for ten. Culture shock connected us, hormones made it fun, and then time ended it all – thankfully.

Change is frightening, exhausting, and stressful, but it is also exhilarating. No one likes to go it alone, but there are times when we need to. I would have gone through perimenopause wherever I was in the world. It could have been a bit easier if my choices hadn't resulted in so much stress – I had changed countries, partners, and titles at the same time hormones had me changing shape and way too many feminine hygiene products. However, the choices I made gave me some of the most memorable and wonderful years of my life, and if I could do it again, I would change nothing.

The menopausal years were a crazy time for me. Decreasing estrogen levels result in elevated cortisol levels, which can raise your blood sugar and cause you to gain weight. Carrying around a few extra pounds can raise your blood pressure, which leads to tense muscles. My new partner suffered from anxiety attacks, which added to my stress levels and tense muscles. My back, weakened from a break I had as a kid and exacerbated by three years of pregnancy, hurt for a whole decade. The pain spread into my neck and only went away once Yasin and I separated.

Elevated cortisol levels also contributed to everything in my body drying out. My skin was dry, sex required coconut oil and tissues on the bed stand, and I found myself constipated most of the time. I drank lots of water and watched my diet, but shit happens – or in this case, doesn't happen. I developed hemorrhoids.

Dehydration led to tooth decay, so I spent a lot of time and money in a dentist's chair and was horrified at how a broken front tooth changed my appearance. I had Lasik surgery on my eyes, which helped with my distance vision and allowed me to get rid of my regular glasses, but it also changed the way I looked and left me needing new glasses to read.

My hair started falling out.

Everything had me stressed. My parents were ailing when I moved to Australia with my Aussie partner. After a couple of years of moving about the country, we settled in Queensland in a city called Cairns and I found a job that required flying in and out of a remote community every week. Just when I thought we were settled, Yasin decided he wasn't retired after all and got work two states away. I found myself living in a paradise on the weekends, but unexpectedly on my own, while my week was spent working in a remote community with a culture in distress. During the day, I wandered around in a fruitless attempt to get "clients" for my work. At night I slept poorly, listening to screams, drunkenness, and fighting – the sounds of a people in pain.

Then, one Monday morning, I found my body unwilling to move out of bed to make the three-hour flight to work. Fortunately, my neighbour was home and a quick phone call had him coming over, picking out my clothes, making me coffee, and eventually getting me into his car. He gave me short, clear, instructions without judgement; he had suffered depression and seemed to know exactly what to do. We spoke little as we made our way to the grassy bank of a river in the next town, where he had arranged to have me meet with a friend of his who did acupuncture. He put needles in me and told me to sleep, so I did.

An hour later, I was surprised to find myself lying on the bank of a beautiful river, drunk with happiness. I had been so disconnected and sad just an hour before, but now I felt as though a plug had been pulled and all the sorrow and sadness had been drained out of me. My body had not whispered but rather shouted at me to take a break, and this time, I listened. I wanted to be taken care of for a while. I quit my job, flew to Darwin, and got on a bus to be with Yasin.

I am no artist, but as I settled in, I began painting dark abstracts on palm tree fronds. It was therapy for me, but Yasin must have taken it as a sign that I was bored. One day, he came home from his job as a social worker and asked if I would mind spending a night in the local hospital with a newborn Indigenous baby.

"Excuse me?" I said. "I most certainly would mind!" I did not feel strong enough to involve myself yet again in the troubles of the world. I thought back to one of the communities I had worked in where there had been a baby who had died of neglect. She was a beautiful child who everyone loved. I had seen different community members carrying the child around at different times, and I had even held the delicate little one myself at one point. What I hadn't known at the time was that although everyone had loved her, no one – myself included – had taken responsibility for her. She seemed happy enough as she didn't cry; I hadn't considered that this was probably because she was too weak from lack of food and water. She eventually, quietly, passed away. I knew it wasn't my fault, but if it wasn't, then whose fault was it? This was just one event in a series of events that I was taking a break from, and yet here Yasin was, asking if I would step up and care for a child at a time when I was struggling to even take care of myself.

"No," I said. "Ask someone else."

"There is no one else," he replied. And that is how I ended up in a hospital somewhere in Western Australia, taking care of a tiny, whiny, Indigenous baby.

When I arrived, a nurse took me to a spotlessly clean two-bed ward with a chair, a big bed for me, and a little one for the baby. "You can sleep or read or do whatever you want," she said, placing the smallest bundle of life I had ever held into my arms. "It is just policy that we have someone with the newborn, and the mother is unable to fulfill that responsibility at this time." Then she left without another word.

I had never seen anything so small, or so odd-looking. I felt awkward, uncomfortable, and truly not qualified to spend time with something so delicate. My babies had been at least twice as big as this poor infant. They'd had healthy pink faces and cried lustfully. Even after a long, difficult labour with each one, I felt stronger and less, well, confused than I did caring for this package.

The nurse had told me I could just put him in the cradle and go about my business. "Let him cry," she had said. "He will cry most of the night no matter what you do." But he didn't really seem to cry at all; it was more of a pathetic whimper, as though he already had the weight of the world on his little shoulders. I couldn't put him down, so instead I went to find some place where I could make up a bottle and change his nappy.

I spent the night trying to get this strange-looking baby to stop crying. I am not good at that. I like my sleep and didn't appreciate spending the night making up bottles that the child refused to accept and trying to get the bath water to just the right temperature to calm him down. I changed a few nappies, and each time seemed more disgusting than the last. I walked the halls, rocking the child and singing softly. I did no reading or lying about, and I certainly didn't get any sleep.

In the morning, a nurse came in to see how we had gotten on. "Not well," I admitted. She took the child and sent me off to shower and get dressed. When I returned to the lobby, I found another lady holding the child I had spent the night with. I went to her and explained that I was ready to take over again just as the nurse came back and dismissed me. "You can go home now," she said.

"I don't mind," I said. "I can spend the day."

"Thank you so much, but we are good now. Janie will care for the baby until the mom gets back on her feet or we find a foster home."

"I can help," I insisted. I couldn't believe I was offering to do more. I was exhausted, but something had happened during the night: I had fallen in love. Somehow, magically, hormonally, this child had become a part of me that I was not going to give away so easily.

"I feel responsible for this baby," I explained to the nurse. "Please, can I stay with him until you sort something out with the mother? I feel a connection with him now."

"Which is exactly why you may not spend any more time with him," she said, guiding me toward the door of the hospital. I went home and cried as though I had lost a child.

The next day, after eleven months of being period-free, my menses returned and I was back on the hormonal rollercoaster. But this time, the ride made me smile. I was beginning to understand that it was just a part of life, and while I couldn't prevent it from happening, I could be more graceful in my acceptance of it. A lot of what goes on inside us is magic, manipulated by our nature. Medicine and science can explain some of it, but not everything. Our bodies are amazing machines, but they require good care and regular servicing, and they come with an expiry date.

Menopause takes time, but when it is over, we will have turned the page to reveal a new chapter. At sixty, I have taken the time to reflect on all that I experienced and maybe learned a few things. My fifties were a full-on adventure, and I expect no less from my sixties. While I now understand that I might not plan as much, I can be open to the things that happen to me.

If you are truly alive, you spend most of your time either falling down or getting up. Life is an adventure – it can be confusing, stressful, painful, delightful, and rich. And if we want to truly enjoy it, we need to be kind, mostly to ourselves.

I put a photo of me at five years old on the wall where I can see it each morning. I gaze at that little girl and demand that I be kind to her that day. Planning for the future might be near-impossible, and even a little bit crazy, but I can choose to give her a good day, or not. That much I can control.

About Jocelyn Johnston

 Jocelyn (Crabb) Johnston is the parent of three boys, and is a teacher and traveller. She received her master's in education from the University of Calgary at forty-five and then went on to find work in a variety of obscure places including Hartley Bay, BC; LaCrete, Alberta; Ilo, Peru; Saltillo, Mexico; three different parts of the Sultanate of Oman; and a variety of remote schools in the Northern Territory of Australia.

Jocelyn still travels on her Canadian passport – taking on a variety of short teaching contracts – but she currently spends most of her time moving between Australia and Mexico. She has published two children's books: Ozzie Goes to School, published by Harper Collins, and James and the Crocodile, available online. Her newest book, Oman, Oz and Menopause, will be available in April 2020.

Facebook: Jocie's Books

13

A Recipe for Vibrant Beauty

by DeeAnn Lensen

"The Lord did not people the earth with a vibrant orchestra of personalities only to value the piccolos of the world. Every instrument is precious and adds to the complex beauty of the symphony."
Joseph B. Wirthlin

A Recipe for Vibrant Beauty

By DeeAnn Lensen

No matter how simplistic it sounds, feeling good about ourselves and looking vibrant go hand in hand. Notice that I didn't say looking perfect; I didn't even say looking pretty. Vibrant women have a zip in their step, a smile on their face, a rested twinkle in their eyes, and a glow in their skin. And who doesn't want to spend time with that person? We unconsciously crave vibrancy in ourselves, and in those we associate with; it's nature's way of helping us choose mates and determine if someone is safe to be around. Humans would need to turn into robots in order to ignore this function of our primitive brains.

The good news is that many of the ingredients to achieve vibrancy are already at your fingertips. It has less to do with whether we have celestial-quality facial features and more to do with recognizing how our spiritual connection, our thoughts, and everything we put in our mouths and on our skin matters. The ingredients are a triumvirate of spirit, mind, and body – in that order – and through combining them, you can learn to more consistently become the thriving, vivacious person you are meant to be. As you read through my recipe for being beautifully vibrant – one that I created after learning these lessons the hard way – I am hoping that these words will spark your curiosity about yourself and help you get a peek at your potential.

The Self-Care Hamster Wheel

Taking care of ourselves used to be a lot simpler once upon a time, but then came the fear-based marketing trolls. These marketers make a full-time job out of telling us that we're only valuable if we buy their product. As a result, we are constantly being bombarded by airbrushed photos of perfectly-posed young women who we can never hope to compare to. We are shamed for not looking twenty-five. We are shamed for not measuring up sexually, and then shamed for being sexual. If we buy into this, if we're unaware of the manipulation, we are taken advantage of and spun in circles as we try to feel and look good.

I myself got caught up in this mess, trying anything and everything both at once and in sequence in the hopes of being my "best self." I've gone through stages where I felt like I was spinning on a hamster wheel, jumping from one thing to the next in an effort to improve myself. However, reading a book or watching a video rarely incites permanent change. In his book *The Good Life*, my friend Jesse Dylan explains this beautifully:

"Most of us buy diet and fitness books in the hope that a healthier body will give us the energy and enthusiasm we seem to lack. When we see no change in our energy, we buy inspirational books about the secret to happiness and finding meaning in our lives, and then focus on trying to apply those lessons in isolation from an exercise program or good diet. Then we read about building better marriages, or generating material wealth, or finding our purpose in life, and we don't see how they relate to each other. And each time we pick up a new title, the previous books tend to recede from our memory as we focus our attention on the health topic at hand. When we glimpse things in narrow, disconnected fragments ... we get inconsistent results to match."

All of this changed when my coach, Mark Fournier, taught me that my daily habits had created my current platform of existence. This meant that I would never stick to my goal unless I changed the habits associated with it. Through being coached and then coaching others, I narrowed down what worked and then applied it to my own life. What I discovered is that the daily habits necessary to create the joyous, vibrant life I craved needed to be sculpted using three things: spiritual connection, mind work, and simply giving my body what it needs – and only what it needs. Once I put these practices into place, I finally went from mediocre, self-disparaging self-care to nurturing my vibrance.

Ingredient One: Spirit

A beautiful reminder that we are not just a bag of bones with a computer on our shoulders comes from watching our bodies heal. For example, I scratched my arm working in the garden one day and was fascinated by how my arm first told me to recoil to avoid more injury, then went into action to turn the blood into scab and heal the wound – all without my thoughts or permission. Who did that? Spirit! When we can tap into our spirit, into God's consciousness, anything is possible. Not wanting to be a part of organized religion is no excuse for disconnecting from your spirit. People call this power by many different names – God, spirit, the universe, and more – but many agree that embracing it brings powerful peace and opportunity into your life.

Whenever I am faced with a quandary, I first ask God for answers, and then I shut up and listen without ego. I don't always like the answer, but I've learned to be honest about what I hear. When we are void of soul messages, we become a slave to ego, which can also be defined as "Edging God Out." That's where winning at all costs takes priority and relationships get left behind.

Another way I embrace spirit is by copying a practice taught by Dr. Wayne Dyer. Every morning, the first thing he did was to pray and say, "Thank you, thank you, thank you!" Then he asked God, "How may I serve?" He says that what you pray for is what will be mirrored back to you. So, if you pray and ask to be given things, your state of lack is mirrored back to you by the universe and your lack will actually increase! How wonderful it is to have "How may I serve YOU?" being mirrored back instead. I've also embraced another method of prayer that I learned directly from Bob Proctor. He too shared that we should never pray in the negative – focusing on what we don't want in life – as it sends a message to the universe of neediness. Instead, pray, "I am happy and grateful for [your request here]." Not only does this send a more positive message out into the universe to be reflected back to you, but it also plants and reinforces the goal in your mind and can be the sprout of new, empowering habits.

Ingredient Two: Mind

Most people I have encountered have had a skewed understanding of the law of attraction. They believe that we attract what we want simply by putting that desire out into the world, but that is only one of the laws. We also attract what we are; who or what we are "being" in this life is what we get more of. For example, whenever I feel that there is not enough joy coming into my life, I can also see that I am not sending it out into the world.

In order to improve our state of mind, we need to face the programming we learned in our childhood that has set us up to believe we are "worth-less." Personally, I was bullied a lot as a child – as someone of Spanish and Mexican descent who grew up in Utah, I didn't fit in with the rest of my peers. As a result, I became ashamed of who I was. It wasn't until I shone a light on this quiet monster through coaching that I was able to loosen its grip on me and learn to reprogram my thoughts.

Shame is a feeling that every human will experience, and yet most people avoid talking about it. That's a big problem, because shame grows in the dark. If we instead explore these feelings and shine a light on the self-esteem goblin that lives inside of us, feeding off of that shame, then we can learn to sidestep the shame-based fear and make the first move toward stepping into our real worth. Remember, you are never alone in these feelings – after all, society has long used shame to control people. In fact, we tend to judge people more harshly in areas where we feel ashamed about ourselves.

So, what can you do to reprogram yourself and rid yourself of shame? Talk with an empowerment partner, a coach, or an empathetic friend who will hear you out and take a detached look at your situation. Weighing and measuring your shame, self-doubt, and fear is the first step toward nullifying its power over your life, opening the door for the creation of an action plan made up of empowered thoughts and habits.

Ingredient Three: Body

Once your spirit and mind are in alignment, the next step towards achieving vibrancy is to take care of our bodies. My best results were achieved when I stopped trying to guess what supplements I needed and began working with Dr. Mark Rosenbloom of Life Force Med, a renowned anti-aging expert. He did a complete work-up and recommended specific, targeted solutions based on his pillars of wellness – nutrition, exercise, hormones, supplements, and mindset – and the results were spectacular! I've already talked about mindset above, so below I will share some of my learnings around the rest of the pillars.

When it comes to nutrition, Dr. Rosenbloom reminds us to pay close attention to the food we put into our bodies. "Most of us eat because we are either hungry or because it gives us pleasure," he says, "when in truth we should be eating for fuel and nourishment. Those who learn to see food as either fuel or poison tend to make better food choices." Get prepared for success, and start with noticing how foods make you feel. I noticed that grabbing a handful of crackers in the afternoon made me tired afterwards, so I began making lovely veggie platters at the start of the day. That way, they would be ready to eat when I needed a snack, helping me to avoid temptation and break the habit of eating high calorie fast foods in a hunger-driven afternoon rush.

As for exercise, I used to put it off by saying I didn't have time or that I couldn't get to a gym. Then I read that one of the biggest losses of autonomy in seniors comes when they don't have the leg strength to lower themselves to the toilet, and I quickly decided that this was NOT going to happen to me! I also realized that there is no excuse to not exercise – all I need is a space on the floor, a few weights, and some really good CDs that explain how to exercise safely. And I have already seen the benefits of incorporating more exercise into my life – the increase in strength and decrease in back pain is no joke. However, as Dr. Rosenbloom reminds us, "not all exercise is created equal. In fact, some exercise can harm. Therefore, it is critical to become knowledgeable in this area if you intend to gain maximum results and avoid doing more harm than good."

Another way to support our body is through hormones. Dr Rosenbloom shares that "hormones are possibly the most poorly understood aspect of our physical well-being. And yet hormones impact nearly every bodily function, from our emotional states to how well we sleep, from our level of concentration to our memory, from our sex lives to our weight, and even the rate at which we age!" Our bodies thrive on the hormone levels we have at thirty years old, but those levels decrease over time, causing a myriad of problems. Bio-identical hormone replacement therapy can make a significant impact on our quality of life as we age – personally, I was able to skate through menopause through the use of these hormones, and I continue to thrive on them today. It's important to note that past studies have shown that conventional hormone replacement therapy has significant risks – this is because they use patented synthetic hormones, which do have the potential to be toxic. In contrast, bio-identical hormones give the same benefits with far fewer risks. If you are interested in hormone therapy, make sure you see a trained professional who can help you determine what hormones you would benefit from and give you a safe and targeted treatment plan that addresses your specific concerns.

The final pillar of wellness shared by Dr Rosenbloom is supplements. "Unless you are (properly) growing it yourself," he says, "chances are that the food you eat doesn't provide nearly enough of the nutrients you need to thrive. As such, it is critical for you to enhance your diet with supplements." A comprehensive study done by Donald Davis at the University of Texas proved that even the fresh food that we eat today has fewer vitamins and minerals than the foods from decades ago! Our quest to improve the size, growth rate, and pest resistance of plants has led to a decrease in the amount of nutrients they offer. When you combine that with the "dead" fast foods and sugar-laced garbage we eat, the result is that we need to take supplements to achieve proper balance in our diet. However, Dr. Rosenbloom also shares that "like exercise, not all supplements are helpful. Most mass-produced supplements will actually cause you more harm than good." So, I highly recommend finding a forward-thinking "age-less" doctor, nutritionist, or naturopath who can properly determine what YOU need in what amounts and recommend high-quality supplements that will meet those needs. In my experience, when I was thoroughly assessed and put on supplements that met my personal needs, my energy went through the roof.

Outside of these pillars of wellness, skin rejuvenation is proven to be a huge contributor to vibrancy. We are genetically programed to like glowing faces. We are also subconsciously slightly repelled by skin that is rough, flaky, chalky, or looks infected or diseased in any way. In fact, we are less repelled by fine lines than by a lack of grooming! Thankfully, everyone can have glowing skin – it just takes a little bit of care.

Exfoliation (the removal of dead skin cells) is one of the more important steps you can take to achieve glowing skin, and also one of the quickest fixes to create vibrancy. There are three key methods for exfoliation: acids, enzymes, and scrubs. Avoid scrubs that contain nut shells as they cannot be ground perfectly round and tear the edge of the pore. Also, if you have any visible redness or dilated capillaries at all, never scrub your face. This can damage fragile skin, and there are safer options that are much more effective.

You also need to take care when using acids. Alpha hydroxy acids (AHAs) and retinoids – which are commonly used for exfoliation – can be very powerful, and if over-used they will thin the skin beyond repair. For home use, I prefer a lactic acid serum with enzymes three times a week at night. The lactic acid loosens old/dead skin cells and the enzymes "digest" them, typically without the heat, redness, and burns that stronger AHAs can generate.

Exfoliation must be followed up with a serum and moisturizer made of high-quality ingredients that are proven to rejuvenate and hydrate your skin. Through research, I've found that the best option is to use serums with ingredients that are as natural as possible, but are also boosted with carefully-chosen cosmeceutical ingredients. Tweaking natural ingredients and infusing them into a delivery system that will help them work is key. For example, Vitamin C, when grafted with other ingredients, can then effectively eradicate free radical damage and fight wrinkles and hyperpigmentation. Similarly, proteins can dramatically reduce wrinkles and firm the skin when they are made into a peptide. Moisturizers are needed, but it's your serums that are the real "face enhancers." Take the time to find a product that feels good on your skin and targets the concerns you are wanting to address. Also, remember to change up your serums with the seasons – it gives your skin a wakeup call!

Putting it All Together

Now that we have the ingredients for our recipe, we need to implement them in our day-to-day lives to ensure that these goals don't become fads that quickly fade away. Imagine how vibrant you will feel and look when you embrace these tools permanently.

One of the reasons we set goals and don't achieve them is that we create our goals using the conscious brain, but our habits are driven by our subconscious brain. If we don't work to change those subconscious habits, we won't stick to the plan long enough to enjoy the results. The method I use to change my habits is to write down my goal, create a vision of the results I want to achieve, and constantly track my progress. For example, in order to help make exercise a daily habit, I created a workout calendar with space to write what workouts I did each day, along with a picture of a place we were planning to visit on an upcoming Mexico trip and one of me at my fittest – I want to feel strong and confident on this trip, so this provided needed motivation. I also tracked my strength, fitness levels, and waist measurement so I could see how I was progressing towards my goal. What gets measured gets done.

Another way to help change your habits is to get other people involved. Last January, my husband, my daughter, her partner, and I all went on the Whole 30 diet – an extremely restrictive but profoundly healthy thirty-day regime. This can be a very challenging diet to stick to, but the four of us were able to stay on course because we could share recipes and success stories. In fact, sharing this ritual with people I love made it a fun experience rather than the difficult slog that it could have been.

Conclusion

As it turns out, cooking up vibrant beauty is ultimately a lot less work than letting myself down, which is what I was doing when I didn't practice fully directed self-care. The most dramatic, shocking change I have ever seen in myself came when I embraced a full, balanced wellness regime that incorporated spirit, mind, and body. You deserve these same results – it just takes a new approach. So, get off the self-care hamster wheel and take a good look at the habits that are driving you, as they are creating your reality. If you feel that your current thrive quotient doesn't meet what you desire, then take steps to connect with spirit, learn let go of shame, reprogram your mind, and take targeted care of your body. Once you do, your vibrancy will astound you!

About DeeAnn Lensen

DeeAnn Lensen is an award-winning, European-trained Advanced Aesthetic Educator, Spa Consultant, Certified Life Coach, NLP Practitioner, keynote speaker, and #1 bestselling author. She is the president and CEO of Touché Beauty. She also owns Advanced Spa Technologies, a five-star spa consulting, education, and distribution company in Canada.

A pioneer in pairing empowerment with spa treatments and spa staff education, her multi-faceted strengths have empowered thousands from the inside out. Frustrated by the onslaught of fear-based marketing targeted at women, DeeAnn dissected the cosmetic industry with its own fine-tooth comb and created Emotional Freedom Technique tapping exercises for women to use while applying skincare to increase self-compassion. She also offers many public programs, including the "Empowered Inside Out Support System: Emotional Intelligence/Life Coaching." DeeAnn also offers "Emotional Freedom Technique Downloads" and "Women's Empowered Inside Out Evenings and Event Speaking."

As a successful spa consultant, DeeAnn has advised spa properties across North America and consulted many companies on skin care product development. She is deeply respected for her ability to support spa businesses through education, creative marketing, empowering staff and coaching management, as well as speaking at Empowered Inside Out seminars for the clients of the spas she supports.

www.DeeAnnLensen.com
Facebook: DeeAnn Lensen/Empowered Inside Out
Email: dee@lenseninc.com
Phone: 604-916-8354

14

Your Health is in Your Hands ... and Your Hips!

by Janice Benna

"Let's kick up our heels and GET GLOWING."
Janice Benna

Your Health is in Your Hands ... and Your Hips!

By Janice Benna

Have you ever wanted to do something but talked yourself out of it with comments like "I need to lose weight first," "I am too old," "I am not pretty, sexy, coordinated, talented enough," or "maybe when the kids are grown up"? Sadly, women seem to have a keen ability for being too hard on themselves. After all, who *doesn't* have body issues or trouble with self-confidence? I have had my fair share of insecurities throughout my life, and while I haven't completely gotten rid of them, there have been significant shifts. It is my hope that through this chapter, I can help you spark a desire to begin loving yourself more and rid yourself of the shackles of self-doubt.

Growing up, I had a Jennifer Lopez body in a Farrah Fawcett era. The 1980s was a time of blondes and thigh gaps, and yet there I was, a short redhead with thighs that clung to each other like their lives depended on it. There's nothing like being a "carrot top" in a time when it was socially acceptable to mercilessly tease and bully people who didn't conform. I honestly thought no one would ever find me attractive because it seemed like everyone at school hated my hair and freckles. I felt like a freak. The only people who seemed to compliment me were nice, elderly ladies – not exactly the dating demographic I had in mind for myself at twelve years old. My mom constantly told me that I was beautiful and that she would "kill to have my figure," but her compliments fell on deaf ears. I figured that as my mom, she HAD to tell me that kind of stuff. Besides, while I thought my mom was beautiful, she never seemed to like her own body. After watching her attend Weight Watchers on and off throughout my childhood, I absorbed a lot of that "I am only happy with myself when I am thin" mentality.

Looking back now, I can see that I really just wanted to be seen and valued by myself – and for boys to notice me, of course! However, I didn't have any idea how to make that happen. When I fell in love with my first boyfriend at fifteen, I figured I'd made out like a bandit because I could not imagine other boys desiring me. It wasn't until I reconnected with an old friend years later that I learned all the guys in my group of friends had been attracted to me. There's a REALLY good chance you have secret admirers too, so don't doubt your value and attractiveness for a second.

Life was good in the years following high school. I married Mike, my high school sweetheart, just three weeks into being twenty-two. Our first daughter was born in 1994, and four years later we welcomed our twins. Then, when the twins were about two years old, I discovered a local women's Can Can dance troupe and decided to join. I had taken ballet as a kid

– just Saturday morning classes at a recreational centre, not one of those fancy ballet academies, but they had still created a love of movement, music, and posture that had been forgotten over the years. Rejoining the world of dance as an adult felt both terrifying and exciting, but once I got going I had SO much fun. I made new friends, learned new things, got a great workout, and had time that was just for me.

Eventually, I got to the stage where I was ready to perform, at which point those old insecurities flared up again. What if I messed up? What if I embarrassed myself? What if I let the other ladies down? What if I was JUDGED? My first gig was at a seniors' care home, so it wasn't exactly a high-pressure environment. However, that did not keep my kneecaps from jumping up and down and my heart from beating out of my chest. Thankfully, the performance went pretty well, and I was hooked. The costumes were so colourful and fun, and being in front of an audience was exhilarating.

I stayed with that group for quite a few years, and during that time I grew both as a dancer and a woman. There is something about being on stage or in costume that makes others treat you differently. People feel special if you make eye contact with them while performing. Then, when the performance is over, they want to talk to you and take pictures with you. It felt a bit like being a rockstar. In those moments, I would completely forget my worries about my weight; there's no time for that when you are posing for pictures and entertaining the masses!

Sadly, while I was finding my groove with dance and being a mom, my marriage began deteriorating. My husband was a good man in many ways, *and* he was also a workaholic. He would be at work eighteen hours a day, seven days a week, basically leaving me to run the house, raise the kids, and live like a single mom who couldn't date. I lost myself in the relationship for awhile, and it was a very lonely time for me. I found one of my callings in raising my children, and that helped. Unfortunately, though, my husband's idea of "helping" was to critique me so I could improve. Cue additional self-image problems! Finally, after twenty-five years together (seven years dating, seventeen married) we divorced in an eight-year long blur of heartbreak, stress, and hurt.

Then, about four years into the divorce, I was diagnosed with multiple sclerosis (MS). I had been having odd symptoms, such as taking two-hour naps every day, parking my car off-centre, mentally feeling "wonky." An MRI showed a white mass at the base of my brain, which prompted the diagnosis. This was traumatic for me, to say the least. At first, I raged at how much time I had lost to the ugliness of the divorce – the ruined holidays, the stress clouding my time with the kids, and the lost opportunities to have wonderful, happy memories. I was dating a lovely man at the time, but the divorce drama and the diagnosis was just too much for me. So, I ended the relationship. Then, I got down to the business of repairing myself and my life.

Unwilling to accept my "fate," I fought my way through all the fear and worries and began digging into documentaries about health and healing. I ended up doing a raw green juice fast for two weeks, and in that time all of my symptoms cleared up. I have stayed on a plant-based diet ever since, and I have had zero progression over the last seven years. I also took the attitude that I had been misdiagnosed, because I felt that if I believed it to be true, then it was true.

After switching to a plant-based diet, I realized that the ethics of not consuming animal products sits really well with me. I also came to recognize that the MS diagnosis was a gift, because it showed me that my self-care was WAY off. I now have a team of grounded, lovely, excellent alternative caregivers, including a homeopath, a naturopath, a counsellor, and of course my solid, reliable girlfriends. These ladies have guided me, supported me, educated me, and kept me calm and focused on what matters. I also was able to find a life coach, who has been a godsend. She was able to redirect my thinking away from anxious, looping, fear-based thoughts and show me how I can see stressful situations differently, communicate better, and care for myself more. She was someone I could really open up with and let my vulnerabilities be out on display. To this day, I credit her teachings for keeping me sane and allowing me to enjoy life so much more than I used to.

During all of this upheaval, I stepped away from dance for awhile. However, once my life settled back down a bit, I was asked by a friend to create a surprise burlesque routine to be performed by the two us as well as a couple of our mutual friends at her wedding. I was somewhat experienced at doing group choreography and music editing, so I jumped at the chance to do this for her. It was a life preserver during a rough time. I started to see my talent in creating routines – I could see movement, patterns, and steps when listening to the song – and having that creative outlet really helped me hold myself together. After the wedding, the other ladies told me they'd had so much fun learning this new routine and were missing getting together and performing. They encouraged me to start my own group, and with that, Hourglass Cabaret was born!

I have taught other women to dance, perform, and find their inner sex kitten for many years now. We've gone from that one wedding routine to having a dozen routines in our pocket, with more on the way. And we don't just stick to burlesque – we dig into a variety of styles including country line, showgirl, musical theatre, disco, and more. We donate our performances and time at charity events, and in doing so, we spread the good vibes and feelings we get from being connected by dance and purpose. We make no money, just good memories, and we leave with the knowledge that we have done some good in our little neck of the woods. It's had its ups and downs, side-to-sides and two-steps, but I still get a "kick" out of it! I've received a lot of positive feedback from members who found an aspect of themselves they had forgotten about or didn't even know was there, just like I had when I first came back to dancing all those years before. I receive thank you notes from dancers for the support and guidance they received, and for providing them with a safe and fun place to escape to on Monday nights. They tell me they always feel better after dragging their tired ass to practice. This is why I do it – this is why I teach.

I honestly don't know what I would do without dance, so I have no plans to stop. I want to be a crazy little old lady still dancing up a storm and causing trouble at the old folks' home, and my friends who dance plan to do the same. We joke about "geriatric lap dances" and needing knee pads for some of our routines down the line. Heck, even now some of us lightheartedly groan and complain about certain moves, but that never stops us from doing them!

Life is not always what we plan for; it is what happens and how we react to it. Had you asked me back in my twenties what I would be doing at my current age, I would have told you I'd be enjoying my grandkids with my husband and travelling, or at least planning for it. Instead, I have reinvented myself as a single mother, dance instructor, and performer. I have been dating younger men (I think I would wear out an older man), travelling with my youngest daughter, performing, teaching, and modelling a bit for friends. I am now in a loving relationship with a man who is a live-by-example, old-fashioned darling of a human who loves my curves and my kids. And now I sit here, trying to put on paper the million or more minuscule and massive turning points and lessons that have brought me here, hoping more women can find this treasure I now possess.

As I have moved down the curvy road and through the peaks and valleys of finding my body positivity through life traumas, coaching, and dance, I have learned to love myself exactly as I am. My body image was terrible for most of my life, which is ridiculous because I now look at pictures of myself when younger and wonder how I ever saw myself as fat, unattractive, and flawed. I have fought HARD not to pass these same insecurities along to my kids, and I think I have mostly succeeded, although only time will tell. They are adults now, and they all seem to have a pretty solid self-image.

I also cannot emphasize enough the importance of finding something that lights you up. For me, it is dance and sex/sensuality. Dance has played an incredibly important role in my life; there is nothing like moving in joy to make you forget your age, body image, and any other issues. Music is therapy, movement is therapy, and being aligned with those around you is therapy. Don't get me wrong, I'm not saying dance class is a substitute for counselling or psychiatric care, but it might just be the shot in the arm you need to feel good.

As for sex/sensuality, that really came to me when I was in my thirties. Even though my life was falling apart around me, I began to feel more solid in who I was and as I lit up sexually and my confidence soared, I found myself and I got grounded. I think a lot of women come into themselves more in their thirties. Then our forties arrive, and we stop caring so much about what others think. This makes it so much easier to embrace ourselves for who we are.

Those who know me know that my brain is always looking

for opportunities for innuendo, flirtations, and outright scandalous comments. My poor son has had to endure a lot of hysterical laughter from his friends while he just shakes his head! In reality, though, my open attitude (along with healthy respect and boundaries, of course) has helped all three of my kids hold their bodies and sexuality near and dear to them, allowing them to make informed choices about their activities and partners with no shame.

I have also learned that movement – whether it is taking a step forward in life, shifting perspectives, or doing a sexy hip circle – is what we all desire. It is what brings change to our minds, expectations and bodies, not to mention igniting the flames of passion and sensuality. I believe this is where a woman's inner glow comes from – that goddess light that society tried to extinguish eons ago.

Women are often expected to place the needs and wants of the people around us far above our own. I have come to realize that we don't lift others up by weighing ourselves down. We have been sold a pack of lies about our worth and looks by people who benefit from us allowing ourselves to be small. Have firm boundaries with others – give them time, generosity, and your glow to light their way, but do not give them your heart and body or let them set up space in your self-image unless they EARN it. I want you to shine like the sun, to be so bright and confident that people need to wear SPF 80 sunscreen just to hang out with you. I want you to hold space for yourself, and to take up space. Don't be afraid of your size or personality – it is okay to love these things! Instead, use your physical, emotional, and spiritual space.

Remember to fill yourself up with things that spark joy, excitement, and sensuality within you – there is no excuse not to. Age does not matter; I am fifty-two and don't really consider it anymore when making decisions. Weight does not matter; I am over two hundred pounds and rocking my curves. Health does not matter; I'm going through menopause but there are no hot flashes yet, just hot dance moves! If happiness is what you seek, then know that it is already inside of you – you just need to find what unlocks that door within.

Through all of this, my life coach Sharon has been one of my most valuable teachers. So many of my most important lessons have come from her, and I know that almost every single one of her clients feels the same way. So, I decided to collaborate with her to put out a "recipe book for a happy life" that will share the key lessons she has taught her clients over the past twenty-five years. This book will be an instruction manual for empowering your life through improving your communication, learning to manage your emotional life, and helping you combat anxiety and depression. I am so excited to be a part of this project as I truly believe it will help everyone lead a happier, more fulfilling life. "Life Skills for All: Recipes of Resilience" will be published in Summer 2020.

I carved my own path to wellness, and I welcome you to follow. I might have created it through my own challenges and lessons, but its significance is not lessened by others walking it. Whether you make your own journey or follow my path, JUST GO. Find your light and beam it out to inspire others. Light a match under yourself and see what happens. Move through this world like you own your body and your being, because you do! Humans are only limited by their beliefs. So, believe you can have what you desire, keep seeing it, and never stop working towards it.

With all my love, Janice

About Janice Benna

Janice Benna is an ethical investor, mother, philanthropist, passionate vegan, dance instructor, and long-time lover of natural medicine, sexuality, psychology, and mental health. She has a strong desire to share what she has learned over the years so that others can benefit from her life experiences.

Dance has been a transformative activity and blessing in her life since childhood – rediscovering it in her early thirties was just what the doctor ordered! Not only did it become a favourite hobby, it was and continues to be a place of learning, growth, connection, and creativity for her. She now shares this opportunity with other women through her women's performance troupe, Hourglass Cabaret. The group is made up of women of all ages and backgrounds; some have danced before, some have not. Their message is to let the music move you, let your inner beauty shine, see your outer beauty, and value/love the body you live in.

Charity work is, in Janice's mind, an elixir of wellbeing. The group gives back to local charities and fundraisers by volunteering and performing at many functions every year.

www.hourglasscabaret.com
www.awomanofworth.com/janice-benna

15

Finding a Way Forward

by Ali Perry-Davies

"Beautiful souls are shaped by ugly experiences."
Matshona Dhliwayo

Finding a Way Forward

By Ali Perry-Davies

When I walked into my Nana's room, the first thing I saw was the long brown couch along the wall to the left. At the end of that couch, directly in front of me, was Nana's matching brown chair. Oh, how I loved to run my fingers across the fabric of that old chair. It was all one colour, with a raised flower pattern made from silky thread that felt so smooth it could have been oiled. Her old oak desk was placed just to the right of her chair, and down the middle of the room was her single bed. I would lie on that bed while Nana sat in her chair, and we and would watch *I Love Lucy* together and laugh until we cried.

Nana lived with us after Granddad passed and she'd had "her stroke," as Mum called it. She didn't move much from her brown chair, and when she did, her one leg would drag across the floor. Nana never said much about that, but she could sure tell a story about "the olden days." She was born in 1887, and I think it is truly remarkable that I personally knew someone who had been born two centuries ago. I am so fortunate that she took the time to tell me her stories about her life on the farm, her trips to the big city, and all her adventures – they shaped me into who I am today.

Nana told me how things had changed so much in her time. She had seen all sorts of things come to be that hadn't even been conceived of when she was a girl – things like electricity, running water, indoor toilets, cars, and planes. She also told me something I have never forgotten: that even more things would change from the time I was a little girl until I became a nana myself. She said that is just how progress works – that once it gets started, it just goes and goes. We learn to adapt, she said, and she was so right.

Nana was seventy-two years old when I was born in 1959, so I grew up thinking that nanas were old – really old. My mum was thirty-five at the time, which was older than most women had babies back in those days, and I think this also matters a bit in terms of how I saw the world. I was raised by women who, when I was a child, I felt were old. Then my parents divorced when I was eight years old and a new woman came into my life, our stepmom Sandy. Blending families can have some challenges, but through the years we have grown to have a beautiful, loving relationship and Sandy has been a great influence in my life.

Over the years, I have come to realize that old women know things. Old women have learned to stand tall when they wanted to crumble. Old women are intelligent and kind and have little time for foolish fancies, as my mum would tell me. Old women know intimately what it is like to hurt another person, and to have to live with that knowledge. Old women know the feeling of being shaken to their core and hurt by another, and they have walked the long road back from heartache. Old women are not to be trifled with.

As for me, I started adult life abruptly when I became pregnant at seventeen. I then got married and tried to navigate a way of life so alien to anything I had known or been taught. I was having a child while still being a child myself, and now I suddenly needed to be the person with the answers. And that is an old woman's terrain, although I didn't acknowledge that at the time.

Life could have been easier for me if I had been more open to input from people with more experience. Mum did all she could to help me out, but I was rather stuck in the mindset that I was a mother now and therefore should have a lot more answers than I actually did. It was a time when having more questions than answers would have likely served me better.

As the years went on, there were two beautiful children, some divorces, college, careers, and – after some time – the realization of a beautiful life plan that my husband Dave and I had spent many years creating. Perhaps this is where the story I want to share really begins: with the plans, and with how things changed when the plans were derailed and I was left wondering who I was.

The time when everything changed came when I was fifty-five years old. Dave and I had been married almost twenty years at this time, and we had carved out a life that was truly all that either of us had hoped for. I had a career I absolutely loved as a disability case manager for an agency which provided supports and services to Indigenous persons living in British Columbia with any type of disability. Dave was getting close to retirement from the Navy after almost thirty years in service. I was about to head into the studio to record an album, and I was also working on two books. I was just getting to the place where I was becoming an older woman – an elder, finally!

On Valentine's Day 2015, we were on our way to an open house – so looking forward to purchasing our first home – when the unthinkable happened. A young woman was in a rush that day, and she became distracted for a moment as she drove down the road behind us. They tell me she had dropped a side of fries onto the back seat floor and had reached back to retrieve them. When she turned around, there we were, the last vehicle in a line of vehicles waiting to turn. Crash! Of course it was fries, I told Dave – they have always been my nemesis. One way or the other, they get me.

That day would change my life – our lives – forever.

Brain injuries are a curious thing. I didn't even go to the hospital because I didn't think I needed to, although the police at the scene apparently tried very hard to get me to go. In the months and early years after the accident, I couldn't hear how my speech had become slurred, didn't see how I staggered when I walked. I knew lights and sounds were horrible for me now, and that words were hard to find. I also cried, a lot, for no reason I was aware of. But really, I didn't remember much from one moment to the next, so these changes weren't as obvious to me as they were to others. It took years of therapies and tests and working hard, really hard, to find my way back to who I was, but there was no real way back. I won't be that Ali again, the one from before the accident. She is gone.

Of all of the side effects of my brain injury, losing music was the hardest to face. It was my one passion, my safe space, but I could no longer cope with the sensations that music created in my brain. I could not play, sing, or listen to music without severe symptoms. I could not even *think* of music without it creating a swirl of dizziness and headaches; the vibration and sounds were more than I could bear. This crushed me. It has taken five years to get to a place where I can play and sing for about thirty minutes, and I am hopeful that one day I will be able to sing with a full band again. For now, I do it all a new way.

While much was lost on the day of my accident, there were also treasures to be found hiding under the rubble. Painting, for one. Through the haze of dealing with my injury, the disability case manager in me must have reached up and grabbed hold of all my previous knowledge of what was required for rehabilitation after an acquired brain injury. I went to the art store, bought some supplies, and began to paint. I had never painted before, but I quickly learned it was a wonderful form of therapy for me. It helped me use my brain in a gentle way and got me out of my head, where I had been trapped in a series of downward spirals that took my thoughts to such a dark place. I started with just two minutes of painting at a time, then five, then fifteen, and within a few months I could paint for an hour before I needed to rest. As I painted, I started to feel like there was hope again.

I was making progress, but I still had so far to go – although the people around me who didn't see me often couldn't always see that, nor could strangers who were meeting me for the first time. Brain injuries are an oddity as many of the symptoms are invisible. For the most part, when people with brain injuries aren't slurring or staggering – which actually just makes us look a tad drunk – we appear rather normal. People would tell me how I inspired them, and I would feel like some kind of fraud. I didn't feel inspiring; I just felt scared and so, so lost. I had lost myself, and I had to find a way back to who I was.

I suppose it was in those difficult moments when it became apparent that if I didn't get up right now and take a step forward,

I would be lost forever. I didn't just have to find out who the new me was, I had to create her. And that's really just a part of life, isn't it? Whether it is an injury, an illness, a relationship, a job, or a wellness regime, we create and recreate ourselves. We start in a new direction, taking one step at a time, and when we fall, we cry and curse and then get up and go again.

So, that's what I did. I got up and went to the brain injury program when I wanted to lie in bed and cry all day. I painted when I could barely stand without falling over. On the days I couldn't stand, I would sit on an exercise ball. Sometimes, I met with a few friends even though I literally could not remember what they said from one sentence to the next, or even what I had said. I just kept showing up. I was so very tired all the time, but I would get up and go for walks and to a variety of rehabilitation therapies. I still become exhausted very quickly – I am really only good for about an hour or so of doing anything – but I push through and keep moving forward, one step at a time.

Retraining my brain has taught me so very much and changed my perspective. Things that I once saw as being so important now seem almost foolish to me. For example, my skin. A few years ago, I looked in the mirror one day and saw that there were jiggly turkey bits under my chin and all down my neck. Now, I can promise you that pre-accident, this would have been an issue for me. Today, though, I look at my face and skin and I love it. Loose skin is a privilege that many are denied.

I have also found that aging with a partner and friends can be comforting. This realization came to me when Dave and I were playing euchre one night with three other couples. We have known this group of friends for over two decades, and together we have gone through births, deaths, marriages, divorces, and so many other life events. Looking around the room that night, I saw the washed-out hair, the silver tips, the gently etched lines, and a few deep crevasses that dug further into the skin. I saw faces weathered by time and worry and gardening and joy, and they were all beautiful to me. As I thought back over the decades we had shared, I realized that we had become worn together, and I saw what a positive thing that was. Perhaps we once were a little quicker to react, a little firmer to the touch, a little more energetic, but we were so much more comfortable with each other now. It is like when our granddaughter Hannah wore out her favourite softball glove, and Dave and I bought her a new one as well as having the old one re-laced. Despite having a new glove, Hannah preferred the re-laced mitt – it felt better, familiar, safe. I am learning that we are at bit like softball gloves; we are such a better fit once we are worn in a bit.

Another wonderful lesson my injury has taught me is to stop answering questions that were never asked. This was a big one for me. So often in life, I would speak before I truly understood what someone was wanting or needing from me. I think at times I saw pauses in a conversation as an invitation to insert my latest opinion and, well, educate.

Today, life with a brain injury means that I am slower at processing things. To help you picture what I mean, imagine that everything you know is in a large, well-organized filing cabinet. Then someone comes and dumps that cabinet out into a room filled with fans, and the papers blow everywhere. Now, imagine that another person asks you a question, and you would like to access one of those files in order to give them an answer. You know the file is still there, that the information is not lost, but you have to sift through all of the paper to find it. As time goes on you can organize the files a bit at a time, but the process can be overwhelming. That's what it's like. Now that

I am dealing with this issue myself, I have learned that people sometimes need space and time to process something, and that jumping in and offering suggestions isn't always helpful. I have also learned to be accepting and kind, both toward others and toward myself.

I had been waiting all my life to be an old woman – a wise being who was unafraid, prepared, and sure of herself. It was to be my right of passage, and then it was gone, and I needed to relearn and reinvent. And in the process, I realized that the stories I had told myself about old women were nothing more than romantic notions. When I was a younger woman, I thought older women had all the answers. The elders in my life always seemed so sure of themselves, without insecurities or wondering, and their answers all seemed so clear. I imagined there would be a time and place in my life when I too would suddenly know the secrets held by the elders, but the reality was so different – so subtle, gentle, and humble. Us old women don't necessarily know things as much as we are satisfied to not have all the answers. We know the difference between a want and a need. We know there is often more value in listening than in talking. We know that questions will likely take us farther than answers, and that there is a huge difference between believing and knowing.

I know now what I could not have known when I was younger – and when I say that, I mean I truly could not have known. Someone else could have figured these things out at a much younger age, but for me, knowing the sacredness of a moment took pain and immeasurable loss. Any given moment could truly be your last, and as scary as that might sound, this knowledge is actually glorious and freeing. There were many times when I said what I thought someone might want to hear or did what I thought they might want me to do, but now those days are gone. As Mum always said, there is no time for foolish fancies. This moment, right now, is the one that matters; no other is promised. So, what will I do with it? Waste one moment, one word, one breath on anything but what is the absolute truth to me? No! When I speak now, I will not waste one syllable on anything but that which is my truth.

I am finally an older woman – stunning, intelligent, kind, powerful, and wise. I am a divine being walking in my truth and appreciating every moment. Hallelujah!

I want to take this moment to speak directly to anyone who has found themselves in a similar situation. Your life has been turned upside down, forcing you to re-evaluate everything you thought to be true, and you may be feeling afraid and alone. My wish for you is that you will find hope for a part of yourself through my story. There is always a way forward, a way to re-invent yourself, and there is always hope. I know it might not feel that way for you right now, but feelings are not facts. As a dear friend once said to me, "Putting off the inevitable only puts off your happiness." You can create a life more beautiful than you could have ever imagined, and you can re-create yourself into the person you have always wanted to be. You just have to find your own way forward.

About Ali Perry-Davies

Ali is a person who is often described as someone who wears many hats. She has worked for many years as a disability case manager, minister, worship leader, musician, writer, and storyteller, creating a wonderful skill set which continues to evolve. After sustaining a brain injury in 2015, she has continued to find new ways to re-create herself. She lives in Victoria, BC with her husband Dave and their German Shepherd Sammie.

Ali has sat on several boards throughout her career, including the Family Support Institute of BC, which supports families with children and other family members living with disabilities, and the Military Family Resource Centre, which supports military families. She has served on Aldergrove and Esquimalt boards as well as the national board for military families, and she has volunteered for over fifteen years performing fundraising for various agencies which are all now under the Community Living BC umbrella.

Ali now spends time creating music, stories, poems, and paintings.

Facebook: Ali Way Art
Instagram: @Ali_Way_Art
Linkedin: Ali Perry-Davies

BECAUSE EVERY WOMAN IS
A WOMAN OF WORTH

Keep Getting WOWed

Join our exclusive FREE Online Book Club, receive updates about meaningful events and new book releases, or find out how to become an author in a future book in the WOW Series. Details about our book club and VIP Author Mailing List at:

www.awomanofworth.com/books

"A Taste of WOW" – Your FREE Book is Waiting

This eBook includes five chapters: one from each book in the original WOW Series, to give you a taste of the powerful and heartfelt writing of our authors. Topics include Moms in Business, Empowered Entrepreneurs, The Power of Collaboration, Life & Leadership with Soul, and Mental Health Matters.

Get your free copy of
"A Taste of WOW" here:

www.awomanofworth.com/books

WOW *ℓ* BECAUSE EVERY WOMAN IS
A WOMAN OF WORTH

About Woman Of Worth WOW Worldwide

Connect. Collaborate. Celebrate. EMPOWER.
WOW is where empowered women join together to make meaningful connections, collaborate for success, laugh and learn, and celebrate their fabulousness. If you're looking for a place where you can belong, with a group of women who will stand beside you and build you up, then WOW is the place for you. The women who are attracted to WOW are the movers and shakers of the world. They are those who want to make a difference; those who believe in the strength of a community, and those who are wanting and willing to support others, both personally and professionally. We call this "Tribe" and our tribe is amazing. If that sounds like you, take advantage of any of our opportunities and see what all the fuss is about.

www.awomanofworth.com

And be part of our Facebook community at
http://www.facebook.com/aWomanOfWorthWOW

Lightning Source UK Ltd.
Milton Keynes UK
UKHW021147130320
360300UK00009B/1666